Swallow the Toad

Swallow the Toad

From Britain to Germany

ABIGAIL DUNN

THE CHOIR PRESS

First published in the United Kingdom in 2024 by
The Choir Press

ISBN 978-1-78963-433-4

Dedication

To the Germans who taught me that there's only one rule you need to know – how to get around all the rules.

A note on the title: "*Swallow the toad*" is a direct translation of the German "*eine Kröte schlucken*". A student of mine taught me this phrase when she was forced to accept that she couldn't get out of paying her gym membership for another ten months, even though she had written to cancel her contract. This phrase can be used whenever you have no choice but to accept something unpleasant.

Contents

⤱

Contents

* *"Armutszeugnis"* is a typical German word in that it's difficult to provide a one-word, exact translation. Translations include: incompetence, certificate of poverty, inadequacy, poor testimony, and indictment. I have opted for "certificate of poverty" as I am talking about education in this section.

Preface

❦

Do you want to live in a country which has been ranked the top rule-breaker in Europe?[1] Do you keep a wad of cash in your house and worship it every day? Do you enjoy having conversations consisting of rhetorical questions followed by insults? Do you like hiring expensive professionals to complete basic, everyday tasks? If you've answered yes to these questions, then look no further, Germany's waiting for you.

In these turbulent times of uncertainty surely Germany, prized for its:

- job security
- strong labour laws
- solid economy
- hard work ethic
- sense of civic duty
- sense of order
- champion planning
- law-abiding and responsible citizens
- affordable health insurance for all
- great social security system
- excellent and reliable public transport service
- laws protecting individuals

seems like a land of opportunities. Although Germany is a sought-after destination for many, the Germany that I have encountered does not live up to its much-lauded reputation. This autobiographical work is designed to prepare you for the chaos and

---

[1] https://www.independent.co.uk/news/uk/politics/angela-merkel-germany-breaks-more-eu-rules-worst-bottom-class-a8198271.html#comments-area

contradictions underneath the assumed order and organisation that give the country its strong image. It aims to help you figure out the rules and regulations in everyday life, which you are just supposed to know, and can then learn to break and bend when no one's watching. After all, it's very important that you should fit in when in Germany.

Remember: Germans need rules. When there are none, there's anarchy.

Are you ready to find out more about typical day-to-day life here? Yes? Then roll up your sleeves and barge on in!

How well do you know Germany?
Questions

Find out how much you know about the Germans with this little quiz! Let Hermann guide you through his orderly and efficient country. Drei, zwei, eins, off you go!

1. If Hermann invited you to a "public viewing", what might you expect?
    a) Getting naked and hanging out with others.
    b) Going to a free art exhibition.
    c) Watching live football in a bar or café.

2. How long does it typically take Hermann to complete a bachelor's degree?
    a) Three years (or six semesters).
    b) Seven years (or fourteen semesters).
    c) As long as he wants.

3. Until 2019, if Hermann was out of work, how would health insurance providers calculate how much he should be paying per month?
    a) Hermann would pay nothing as he's not earning an income.
    b) They would make up a fictitious income of 2,232.25 euros for him. And Hermann would pay back around 16 per cent of that per month.
    c) They would work it out based on Hermann's last salary.

4. When is a Deutsche Bahn train considered as being late?
    a) If it arrives up to five minutes after the scheduled arrival time.
    b) If it arrives up to six minutes after the scheduled arrival time.
    c) German trains are never late!

5. How much does Hermann earn per month if he has a so-called "mini-job"?
   a)   520 euros
   b)   680 euros
   c)   820 euros

6. What does Hermann do to give himself a clear conscience?
   a)   Treats others with courtesy and respect at all times.
   b)   Separates his rubbish diligently when people are watching.
   c)   Apologises for something profusely if he has made a mistake.

7. When does Hermann form an orderly queue?
   a)   When waiting to place his rubbish in one of the many containers.
   b)   At all times.
   c)   When purchasing an ice cream.

8. Why is Hermann afraid of turning fifty-five?
   a)   Because it's the age at which it's nigh-on impossible to be accepted by a health insurance provider.
   b)   Because he thinks he won't find another job.
   c)   Both of the above.

9. On average, how many times does Hermann go to the doctor's per year?
   a) Four times.
   b) Eight times.
   c) Eleven times.

10. Hermann is considered to be pretentious if he does which of the following?
   a)   Boasts about how much he earns.
   b)   Wears elegant clothes.
   c)   Boasts about how much he saves.

11. Which services does Hermann get for free in German banks?
    a) A no-frills account.
    b) Withdrawals from a bank he doesn't bank with.
    c) None of the above.

12. When Hermann meets a graduate in the field of engineering who works as a graphic designer, what thoughts might go through his mind?
    a) Wow! I wonder how someone managed to have the skill and creativity to change fields.
    b) Wouldn't it also be nice to excel in different areas?
    c) Why did this person fail as an engineer?

13. What does having "self-reliance" and "confidence" mean to Hermann?
    a) Telling people explicitly what you need and want.
    b) Having the ability to firmly say "no" when need be.
    c) Standing up for yourself when being bullied by your boss.

14. What is the approximate average monthly pension for a single woman in West Germany?
    a) 950 euros
    b) More than 1,000 euros
    c) 800 euros

15. Hermann likes to make sure he fits in with his fashion. What is he most partial to wearing?
    a   Black or brown leather trousers.
    b) Trousers ending roughly around his ankles with several centimetres of sock visible.
    c) Lots of bright colours.

16. How can you tell whether Hermann is acting out of solidarity?
    a) He doesn't take up freelance work.
    b) He lets his poorer friends drive his expensive car.
    c) He helps out at the local food bank.

17. How many state health insurance providers are there?
    a) More than ten.
    b) More than forty.
    c) More than ninety.

18. What is Hermann's understanding of "community"?
    a) Volunteering in his local town whenever he can.
    b) Being a member of one or more of the 87,000 organised clubs.
    c) Organising free and fun events, such as concerts and dances.

19. How long can Hermann teach at universities on temporary contracts before he must stop or face breaking the law?
    a) There's no such law.
    b) Six years.
    c) Twelve years.

20. How much interest can Hermann typically hope to earn on his savings?
    a) Between 2 to 3 per cent.
    b) Around 1 per cent.
    c) A maximum of 0.20 per cent.

CHAPTER 1

§28 Deutschland. Warum nicht?
Germany. Why not?

❧

I've always been fascinated by foreign languages and cultures, having studied French and German for my bachelor's and then continuing to do a DPhil in German Studies at Exeter College, Oxford. Here I specialised in nineteenth- and early twentieth-century German fiction (more specifically, the representation of the widow. I encountered no merry widows in my research unfortunately, in case you were wondering). Having enjoyed my nine months abroad at Lake Constance teaching English in a secondary school so much I decided to drop French and make German my focus from then on. During my time abroad I was welcomed into the community immediately. Some highlights of my stay included: being invited to a delicious Sunday lunch at an English teacher's house almost every week, having a cheap theatre subscription and going to the theatre on Friday nights with colleagues, dancing on tables at full-moon parties and travelling around the country on my days off. I really enjoyed the variety of landscapes that Germany offers and I was eager to see a lot more at the next given opportunity. So, in my final year of studies, I had grand plans to actually use my languages in my future job with the ultimate goal of inspiring and motivating others to take language learning seriously. It turns out though that this would be very unlikely to happen. When I repeatedly came across jobs such as "German-speaking IT helpdesk support" with a bit of Polish and Russian thrown in on the side and all for a whopping £18,000 a year, I started to despair somewhat. As fond as I am of the UK, language learning is hardly its greatest asset, so as time passed, I looked more and more to Germany as a place where I could put to good use my love of languages.

I'm not alone in looking to Germany as a secure place to build up a new life. The Germany where it is easier to get German citizenship than to cancel a gym membership, it turns out. A documentary aired on ARTE in 2021 revealed that in the five years following Brexit, around 6,000 British Jews in London have applied for German citizenship.[2] In addition to the huge mess that's Brexit, the British government has recently decided to invest £15 million into language teaching at schools, with German as a focus. It appears therefore that Germany is starting to become a more sought-after destination, and the statistics confirm this. Since 2020, Germany is the second-most popular destination in the world for immigration, after the US. Like most of you I'm sure, I had only ever heard good things about German society. It was, and still is, regarded as a country where, broadly speaking, things are fair, people work together for a common good, and things work. There's no shortage of books on this subject. *Why the Germans Do it Better: Notes from a Grown-Up Country*, published in August 2021 is perhaps one of the most recent examples.[3] The arrogant idea that Germany not only does it right, but does it "better", is a prevailing one and not one I can relate to. Instead, in my eleven years of living and working here, I can conclude that the exception is the norm. If you would like to know how and why Germany is a car accident in slow motion, read on.

---

[2] *Des Britanniques Juifs veulent redevenir Allemands*, published on YouTube 9 December, 2021.
[3] *Why the Germans Do it Better: Notes from a Grown-Up Country*, John Kampfner, Atlantic Books, 2021.

CHAPTER 2

§369 Von Pontius zu Pilatus
From pillar to post

ᔣᔕᔢ

It all happened in what seemed to be the blink of an eye, probably because it was. A successful Skype interview in September 2012 with a reputed university in West Germany led to a job offer commencing the start of October. That's right. One month between interview and start date for a post in a new country; and it's not as if a vacant post for an adjunct lecturer at a German university is a rarity. It happens every two years. Such striking lack of organisation and forethought was to be the rule and not the exception I would later learn. Ever since my year abroad in 2000 in the small but stunning city of Constance, I had been looking for opportunities to get back to Germany, so when I was made an offer for a two-year position as an English language instructor, I snapped it up. As it happened, I had no time to reflect on the offer anyway, as I needed to give enough notice at my existing job and find somewhere to live in a new country – a mean feat when you only have a month on your hands. September 2012 was thus spent scouring flats online in a city I'd never even been to and crossing my fingers and toes I'd find a place to live before I arrived.

Luckily, I was more fortunate than my British predecessor at the university, who spent six weeks living in hostels before she found a flat. But like her, I received no assistance from the university in my search for accommodation. At the last minute I found a place that looked OK from the description given in the email, though when it showed up as a garden shed on Google Maps, I was a little apprehensive. With no time left to worry, however, I packed one large and one small suitcase, all that I was physically able to carry, and made my way to the airport. For the first night I had booked accommodation at what used to be a Catholic hall of residence, but for my one and only night there it was being used for a wedding reception. Unbeknownst to me this residence was also situated in the middle of a forest. Typically, the moment I got off the plane and onto the train it started to pour down, thereby serving to reinforce the feelings of doubt I was already feeling about this whirlwind decision of mine. The train was fairly busy, as I'd managed to arrive slap bang in the middle of rush hour, so it took me quite some time to drag my suitcases to an available seat. When I finally came upon what appeared to be a free seat, I saw a young man sitting down next to it, legs sprawled out and wearing a bike helmet over his baseball cap, adamant not to move an inch. Not exactly planning on confrontation as my first means of German communication, I stood the entire way and arrived at my destination, fighting to get off the train while others elbowed their way in, feeling rather worse for wear to say the least.

Things didn't get better. In order to get to the hall of residence I had to get on a tram after the train. No big deal, I thought, surely I have the worst of the journey behind me. Luckily the tram wasn't as packed as the train, so I was a little taken aback when a German male, talking loudly on his phone, squeezes in front of me as I am standing just in front of the doors. I ask him, in my first exchange in Germany, if he would like to get by, as there are some seats further up the carriage. He gives me an anal look and continues to stand so close that I have to step back if I don't want to inhale his neck hairs. I'm fortunately spared the smell of his neck hairs for too long when a very expensively dressed middle-aged woman decides she would like to stand at the front, hence making the man move to a spot behind me. When the charming young man wishes to get off, he barely turns his head, eyes me from the side, and says, "*Ich muss hier raus*" ("I have to get out here"). I remembered that the Germans could be direct bordering on rude, but this left me gobsmacked. I stepped off the tram a few stops later and asked a lady on the street how to get to my destination.

"On foot?" she asked, which is generally not what you want to hear when you have no other option but to walk.

"Yes," I responded.

"Well," she continued, looking me up and down, "if you're definitely going on foot it'll take you about twenty minutes up those paths through the forest," she said, pointing to the end of the street.

So off I went trudging through the forest in the slanting rain with my glasses steamed up, a suitcase in each hand, and a hood that kept being blown off my head by the wind. After what seemed like an eternity I got to a building. Please let this be it, I said to myself through chattering teeth. The building was indeed spectacular, and in my hazy vision I could make out lots of parked cars and signs of life, so my mood started to lift ever so slightly. Upon closer inspection my hopes were confirmed as it became clear that I had reached my accommodation. Now I just happened to remember that I was in room 27, but there was no one on reception to check in with. I really did begin to feel like I was being "sent from Pontius to Pilatus" as the Germans say, even though it's the same person.

I walked around a bit, peering through doors but despite all the parked cars, there was not a soul to be found. At this point I really needed the loo so I made my way down the corridor whereupon I came to room 27, a key in the door and a sign saying "*Willkommen Herr Dünn*", which translates as "welcome, Mr Thin" (it's perhaps worth pointing out that my surname "Dunn" resembles the German "*Dünn*", which means "thin"). I was happy to claim the room as mine and settled in for the evening, not getting a wink of sleep due to the sound of the wedding reception in full swing until well into the early hours, and then, just as I was about to finally drop off, the sound of a mother screaming at her child in the next room. Whatever your daughter has done wrong, I thought, it can't be worse than you screaming your head off at 3 a.m. in a hostel.

I have since learnt that, be it in a supermarket, on the roads, at the top or bottom of an escalator, on the corner of a busy street, Germans have very little idea about what is going on around them. There is no law that states you must bear in mind that you are not alone on the planet. I was only too glad to leave later that morning. As there were once again no signs of life at reception, I left without paying, and I have never heard a word from them since.

CHAPTER 3

§168 Aller Anfang ist schwer in Deutschland

Every beginning is hard in Germany

ᴄᴧᴧᴧᴐ

When I wasn't being elbow- or, wait for it, stomach-barged out of people's way[4], I kept being asked by strangers and friends alike why I was in Germany. "If I were you, I would have stayed in London. It's such a lively city," or "Why didn't you go to Spain or somewhere like that? People are much friendlier and relaxed down there in southern Europe," were some of the most typical reactions. It was bad enough having to justify my decision to all and sundry back in England, but I never thought I'd be having the same conversations with Germans in Germany.

The most memorable encounter of this kind was with an elderly Polish man who had been living and working in Germany for most of his life. One sunny afternoon I was sitting by the river reading and preparing for teaching when a friendly-looking elderly man, with eyebrows so bushy you could almost put them in a ponytail, smiled at me and said I looked very absorbed in my book. We got talking and I found out that he was very lonely; his family lived far away, his wife had sadly passed and despite numerous attempts, he had never really built up a network of friends here. I guess in some way I connected with him immediately. I was so nervous about my

---

[4] Alas I was once stomach-barged out of a man's way. It was summer and he was wearing a tight T-shirt about twelve sizes too small. I got up from my seat to join the queue to get myself a second coffee, when suddenly a man bumps me out the way with his stomach and takes my spot in the queue.

upcoming job, I knew no one in the area and I was waiting for some kind of confirmation that my move was the right thing to do, so I didn't hesitate being open with him. He found it difficult to say goodbye and I also found it sad. When he left, I had a strange feeling of emptiness, so when I bumped into him a week later in my local supermarket, I decided to take the bull by the horns and invite him out for dinner. This marked the start of a nice if unconventional friendship. I'd phone him up once every two weeks to see how he was getting on and to tell him about my job and how I was experiencing life in a new country. We listened to each other's grumbles and were basically a nice sounding board for each other. Over a dinner of "*Pfifferlinge*" (chanterelle mushrooms) he kept telling me, seeing my determination to make my move a success, not to overdo things and let people exploit me. I couldn't really see what he was getting at but I appreciated his words, nonetheless.

At the end of dinner, I gave him a few vouchers that are given to new residents when they register at the town hall. In Germany it is mandatory to register with the town hall when you move. If you don't, you'll have to pay a hefty fine of 1,000 euros. It wasn't until I got back to my flat that I remembered he wouldn't be able to use the vouchers as they have your name on, and if you want to use them you need to bring ID. Oh well, it's the thought that counts I told myself.

CHAPTER 4

§229 Das ist nicht meine Aufgabe!
That's not in my job description!

ᏟᏗᏗᎷ

When you come to Germany, you'll soon realise that you won't need to do just *your* job, you'll have to make sure you can do everyone else's too. My Polish friend had indeed warned me about this in his own way, but the message hadn't sunk in yet. To help you understand how jobs are carried out here, I've divided the German attitude towards work into four distinct categories:

- I can't do my job.
- I won't do my job.
- It's illegal but I do it anyway (this can be applied to all areas of life).
- I hate my job so I'll make you do it.

The list is long, but for the sake of brevity, here are some professions you'll need to be acquainted with: bank clerk, accountant, tax advisor, lawyer, and administrative all-rounder. My job was to teach English language and "Regional Studies" (this translates as all British history from the Romans to the present packed into one semester). This is quite a big deal, especially when you consider that I was only told I'd be teaching history on my first day of the job. Like most naive newbies, however, I wanted to make a good impression so, in addition to developing a knack for getting my top lip stuck in every awkward meeting with new colleagues, I offered a voluntary film class on British history on Monday evenings. News of this got round fast. Most of my introductions to staff members in the department went something along the lines of the following:

> Member-of-staff-who-I-hadn't-met-yet: "Are you offering a film society on British history on Monday evenings?"

> Me: "Yes, that's right. I'm Abigail. Nice to meet you."

> Member of staff: "Could you also show one or two films related to my course?"

Naturally I was a bit lost for words at this point. I couldn't quite work out how I'd tell my students that instead of watching *Beowulf* as planned we'd be watching *My Family and Other Animals*. Had I been in Germany for much longer at this point, I would have responded like a true German "that's not in my job description", or "*das ist nicht meine Aufgabe*". It didn't take all too long to understand that the typical German is rather work shy, to put it mildly, and loves nothing more than to do the bare minimum for a nice, fat pay cheque.

Only a few weeks later I was again taken aback when I saw a huge pile of English literature essays in my pigeonhole. There was no letter, note, or Post-it to tell me what the heck I was supposed to do with them, just a pile of papers from a bunch of students I didn't know and from a course I didn't teach. It transpired that I was to correct them as the literature professor was too important to do it herself. Well, I suppose that seeking my permission first would have involved far more variables than just pretending she didn't think there'd be a problem. To this day, she hasn't as much as said hello to me.

Oh well, I thought, at least I have colleagues in the language department to turn to for moral support. And that, lo and behold, was when I got to know the German "*Beamte(r)*" (civil servant). My two language colleagues, both like human-sized slugs but with less ambition and henceforth to be referred to as "Useless One" and "Useless Two", were "*Beamtinnen*" (female civil servants). German civil servants are a special breed of worker. Germans like to look upon them as a shining example of how workers are well treated in this country; indeed, teachers who are fortunate enough to become civil servants receive a generous salary and a great pension. But what Germans are reluctant to tell you is the following: once they are established, German civil servants, of almost any level, are not only authorised to exercise executive powers beyond those of their equivalent grade colleagues in any county I know of, but are also virtually bullet-proofed from risk of any serious disciplinary measures if their decisions are later proven to contravene the law.

Basically, it's nigh on impossible to fire a civil servant in Germany, and verbally insulting one can lead to a hefty fine.[5] German civil servants also pretty much fall into two categories: fumbling technocrats with zero social skills, or incompetent paper experts trying to mask that incompetence with fronting and posturing. I mean, even Germans themselves make nasty jokes about German civil servants, so things must be bad. Here's an example:

What's the difference between a civil servant and wood?
Wood works.

Useless One was employed on a full-time, permanent contract, taught two days a week and liked nothing more than taking one of those days off, usually when it coincided with a particularly busy period and always in the run up to exams. Fortunately for her she was helped out by the German calendar. In the months of May and June, depending on which federal state you live in, there are a generous number of public holidays that typically fall on a Thursday, the two most significant being Ascension Day and Corpus Christi. So Useless One carefully planned her working days as Thursday and Friday, making sure that should the public holiday fall on a Thursday she might as well take the Friday off as a "bridge day", granting her an even longer weekend.

In Germany holidays are sacred. Fridays are considered as the weekend and Germans believe they have a fundamental right to a summer holiday. For weeks on end over July and August you'll be hard pushed to make an appointment with a doctor or dentist as they close their surgeries to coincide with the school holidays. This is

---

[5] German bureaucrats have found the most imaginative and lucrative ways of shaking you down for ridiculous amounts of money. More on this later.

irrespective of whether they have school-age children or not. In a country reputed for its strong work ethic and solid health system the mind can only boggle at this. This doesn't just happen in practices where there is only one doctor (which for the record is very common), but even where several health professionals work as a team. Instead, you'll find a printed or most likely handwritten notice pinned to the door of the practice telling you the name and address of the doctor or dentist acting as a replacement. This procedure is repeated for the two-week school autumn holidays in October, the Christmas holidays, the Easter holidays, and bridge days.

On why you should be glad that Germany wasn't unified on 29 February

On the one hand, it's great being a full-time employee in the months of May and June; you get helped out by the German calendar and can feel no shame in tacking on a day or two extra just before or after the public holiday as everyone else does it too. On the other hand, however, there is no flexibility should a public holiday fall on a weekend. It will not be moved to the closest Monday. Instead, you just have two days of everything being closed at the weekend rather than just one. The year 2022 was particularly bad with New Year's Day, the first of May and the first day of Christmas (25 December) all falling on a weekend. With such cold logic as this, it's little wonder that everyone walks around with a face like a slapped arse.

In Germany you could shoot a cannon through an office window at 6 p.m. and not hit anyone. It's simply not considered "efficient" to work overtime. Once the clock strikes six you are to switch off your computer and leave the office no matter what the circumstances. It can even be considered *inefficient* to work beyond your allocated hours, as an acquaintance pointed out. The said acquaintance was once pretty chuffed with himself as he'd managed to finish preparing a document to be used internally. When his boss found out he just huffed and puffed. My colleague didn't understand. "But you were supposed to finish this on Friday this week, not Tuesday! *Das geht nicht*" ("That's not on"). In other words, having completed something ahead of a deadline was considered an inefficient way of working.

One afternoon I was sitting in my office waiting idly for the clock to strike six when in stomped Useless Two sporting her usual pair of trousers in <u>that</u> shade of fruit-pastille green. This time she had coupled her fruit-pastille green trousers with a stripy top, and her face was also a sickly shade of green giving her a nice seasick glow. I was tempted to greet her with "ahoy" but quickly thought better of it. She huffed and puffed loudly all the way to her desk, flopped down on her swanky leather chair, pulled out a bunch of dog-eared papers and threw them down on her desk, the sound of which made Useless One almost choke on the yoghurt she had been slurping. It turns out that the head of department, whose breath could knock you down quicker than Mike Tyson and who liked nothing better than to stand extremely close to you, had finally asked her to do what was in her job description and teach a phonetics course, for which she was the course convenor, no less. Up until then, language instructors like me were required to teach phonetics, as the two full-time members couldn't be bothered to learn a new skill after twenty years of doing exactly the same tasks and instead preferred to palm them on to the clueless newbies who flocked in every two years. But this was all about to change and Useless Two couldn't get out of it any longer, even *"das ist nicht meine Aufgabe"* didn't work its charm any more, and boy was she angry.

The weeks that followed were interesting. Useless Two would spend her office hour ignoring students and swotting up on the English vowel sounds; this not being something she was prepared to do in her own precious time. One afternoon she turned to me and in a strange twist of fate said that she found the contents of the course enjoyable and was having fun teaching it. Several weeks passed in this calm and harmonious manner and then, before you could say dental fricative, it was time for the phonetics exam. On the afternoon of the exam as the students were standing outside the exam hall, a member of staff who was invigilating came to tell me that there was a problem.

"Your colleague, the course convenor for phonetics, hasn't prepared an exam so we're going to have to use yours," she whispered to me, the students within earshot.

"Have her students been taught the same information as mine?" I asked, baffled and angry in equal measure (in all four English departments of German universities I worked at, each and every language course instructor taught the content they wanted; there was no common syllabus).

"Well, even if they haven't, we have no choice. They have no exam otherwise."

So, in we go to the exam hall. Once the students are settled in their seats the invigilator announces that due to "administrative difficulties" everyone would be sitting my exam. There were no complaints, not even any huffs and puffs! Useless Two managed to mark her own exams and no more was ever said on the matter.

Writing an exam for a course that I hadn't taught was a sure sight easier than coming up with content for a course that was obsolete, however. Something that was neither written in my contract nor explained to me at interview, but instead sprung on me in my first week was the fact that I would be teaching the final semester of a master's course. As soon as I found this out, I started manically to brainstorm ideas, as, in what was becoming typical behaviour, I had received no indication of what the students had done so far, nor what was expected of them. Relieved to have come up with a plan of action in time for my first lesson, I proudly announce to the small group of students how we are to spend the course. "We've already done that," came the response.

At that point I just froze and had no more answers. In the course of that first lesson, no doubt largely owing to the fact that the students saw and sympathised with my general levels of cluelessness and floundering, they told me that at the end of the last semester just before I joined the university the German "*Magister*" programme had changed to become a master's. This is what I was told, anyway. And there was no syllabus available for this; the only goal was to finish the course with an extended essay about "something". We put our heads together and decided that they would write an extended film review, as they'd pretty much done everything else. In the end everything worked out, but I couldn't help feeling that the academic rigour and quality I had expected to find here were sorely missing.

CHAPTER 5

§358 Es ist illegal aber ich mache es trotzdem

It's illegal but I do it anyway

⊂∽∾⊃

Now, Germans are not exactly known for their creativity and imaginative spirit, are they? But at least they do things properly, or something along those lines. Here I feel we're not giving them enough credit. I mean, every time someone messes up or wants to cover up the fact they don't know something, have made a mistake, or don't want to declare their full earnings on their tax form, the imaginative German emerges. When I was doing substitute teaching at a private grammar school in 2017 alongside teaching at my third university, my boss could be exactly this kind of inventive German, bending the rules to help him along in life while potentially screwing others.

During my job interview for the school, I was told that teachers are freelance and earn 20 euros an hour, but as I have a PhD and was covering at very short notice, I could get 40 euros an hour. Not bad, I thought. However, my French colleague's interview went somewhat differently to mine – she was asked how much she would *like* to earn. She said 36 euros as that was what she was getting at another school. A month later, when it came to handing in my payslip, my boss, otherwise known as Mr Don't-tell-the-taxman, asked me to fill out two forms. One for his records, which said I was earning 20 euros an hour, and one for me, which said I was being paid 40 euros an hour. As a foreigner not yet all too familiar with the ways of Germans, I couldn't help but feel "*verarscht*" (taken for a ride – something which you have to accept as part of daily life here).

I told my students about this a few years later when I was working as a freelancer. I was a little apprehensive when I told them, worried I might be revealing too much, but no one batted an eyelid. "Everyone here finds something to hide or not declare on their forms," was one particularly insightful response. As it turns out, Mr Don't-tell-the-taxman had his justification already prepared. I couldn't possibly declare my full rate on my payslip, as what might happen, heaven forbid, if a colleague on 20 euros an hour sees it? That will just provoke outrage and the common feeling of German "*Neid*", or "envy" in English.[6]

I don't believe that one has had the full-on German working experience, however, until one throws back-stabbing and bullying into the bending-the-rules mix. German employment law does not really have provision for unfair or constructive dismissal, nor for age discrimination, which is one of the reasons why bullying is simply a way of life here. In fact, Germany didn't pass the EU anti-discrimination directive into national law until as late as 2006. It failed to implement this law by 2003, the deadline for EU member states. To this day there are still very few sanctions against bullying and discrimination and many HR departments (or "*Betriebsrate*") have no instruments for putting a stop to it. (At a vocational college where I later worked, for example, the PE teacher took on the extra role of discrimination officer.) HR is virtually relegated to admin roles and rarely assumes any part in conflict or defining the standard code of conduct in the workplace and leaves it to common sense, which is often variants of might-is-right/take-it-or-leave-it and my-turf-my-rule. The happiness or personal development of the individual is an absolute irrelevance, complaining is seen as trouble-making and whistle-blowers are routinely fired. To put this into some kind of perspective, this is how it works in Germany: once you reach the tender age of forty, finding a job gets tough. This is why many Germans pray for that job that'll last a lifetime, as trying to switch jobs or careers is a recipe for disaster. Essentially any job applicant over the age of thirty is considered too old to change careers, anyone over forty wishing to change their job is considered having failed at their previous job, anyone over fifty is considered

---

[6] Everything in Germany can provoke "*Neid*".

incompetent and senile, and anyone over sixty is pretty much half dead anyway. Which is ironic as most Germans finish university around the age of thirty.

When I first came to Germany I thought, rather stupidly in retrospect, that a rule was a rule and that was that. Aren't Germans well known for their love of rules and their parrot-like way of obeying them? That's not entirely true. What they are actually talented at are finding ways around the rules so that they do not have to follow them. It's like not implementing a law against discrimination so you can deal with it or ignore it however you please. To illustrate my confusion, or stupidity, regarding German rules and their implementation, take two-year, non-renewable contracts at universities. Upon arriving in Germany, I believed that if you had a non-renewable two-year contract then the contract couldn't be renewed after two years. When I also discovered that it is not legal to work for more than six years in one "*Bundesland*" or "federal state" on temporary contracts at German universities, I had to reluctantly swallow the bitter pill and face the fact that I'd be looking elsewhere for employment once my six years were up. The laws of the land dictate that you cannot continue to teach at a university in your federal state if you have been working for six years on temporary contracts at universities already. The options you then have are as follows: a) get offered a *permanent* position in your state; b) move to a different state; c) change career paths.

These so-called "*Kettenverträge*" or "chain contracts" have been around for donkey's years and back in the 1980s it wasn't uncommon for employees to sue the university over their employment being terminated, and the courts ruled that because their contracts had been extended a couple of times, they were considered "chain contracts" so people had to be allowed to stay on as permanent employees. At least two people I know who have the fortune to work at universities on permanent contracts sued their respective universities; one because he deemed it unfair that he was doing the same work as permanent staff but had much fewer rights (who knew?), the other as he found a racist clause in his contract. So off to court he went and bagged himself a permanent contract. I suppose that based on this history universities are now reluctant to extend a contract even once. The "logic", as we now know, behind this six-year rule is that universities are legally obliged to give you a permanent contract after six years and this is something they don't want to do. This is to save money of course.[7] But I must say here that this is a particularly fuzzy law (one of many), which even Germans either don't know about or don't fully understand. What makes matters even more baffling is that if you happen to sign a contract before you've taught your first ever lesson, you are entitled to a permanent contract!

Anyway, one day towards the end of my sixth year of university teaching, I was just checking my emails in the semester break when I came upon an email from Ms I-can't-do-my-job who mistakenly sent around the teaching timetable for the next semester. This featured my colleague who also had a two-year temporary contract like me and whose contract was up in the summer just like mine. Why is she down to teach then? I wondered. Something didn't add up here. I immediately wrote back to Ms I-can't-do-my-job copying in the rest of the language department too. The first answer I got from her was extremely illuminating so I'll share it for your benefit here:

Unfortunately, I've sent the wrong schedule.

This was then some days later followed up by Prof. Nothing-in-writing (the head of department) who was adamant to absolve himself of any responsibility in the matter, because clearly this was all that was at stake here:

I hear that some of you are confused by some file (for which I was not responsible) in which X's name appears as an instructor for next semester. I can understand your confusion. This should have been N.N., as it is currently not clear who will fill this position. If you have any questions concerning your contracts, please make an appointment with me in person, and we can talk about it.

The correspondence continues in this vein; me stating that instructor X is indeed rostered to teach in the upcoming semester, it's even published online for all to see for crying out loud, and with Prof. Nothing-in-writing reiterating that he is "*not involved in setting up schedules and putting them online*" and that I am "*welcome to talk about this*" but he "*does not want to discuss these issues via email*". As

---

[7] "*Geiz ist geil*" (cheap is sexy). A true German lives by this maxim.

with most Germans, Prof. Nothing-in-writing is very quick to point out that he is not responsible; it's not his fault, someone else did it.[8]

It is not enough for a German to try to avoid accountability at all costs. Once you have confronted a German for their bad behaviour, they will do whatever it takes to push everything back on you, punish you, and generally make your life a misery. This can take various forms but most typically includes: making a list of the mistakes you have made[9] and turning their anger towards you outwards and seeking to exercise a maximum of control over you. Ms I-can't-do-my-job couldn't wait to get started on me. No sooner had I questioned her about the dubious timetable for the upcoming semester than she presented a form to me detailing the termination of my contract, duly putting me in my place. The final insult resulted in my being asked to sign a clause of "professional secrecy and non-disclosure". In her office on my last day of work I made it very clear that I was not willing to sign this. As I was leaving her office, I heard what at first seemed like the sound of leaves rustling in the wind. I was brought back to reality with a bang when I realised that this was not the poetic sound of nature in the wind I heard, but rather the sound of an angry woman with a lisp hissing insults under her breath at me while I had my back turned.

This sneaky and discreet form of harassment and back-stabbing was taken up a notch at the first university I taught at. There are myriad ways of bending this fuzzy two-year-rule, I learnt, and my new and dynamic colleague was to show me just how it could be done. Mr Lowlife (not his real name – though it does sound very similar) joined the department twenty months into my contract, and was immediately liked and appreciated by all, including Useless One and Useless Two (though this was not reciprocated by Lowlife). As he held a position of some importance at his former university, he took no time in telling others how to do their jobs better and how things should be managed here. No real offence was taken by this –

---

[8] A defining trait of the German character is that of denying any responsibility and avoiding the consequences of actions. This is particularly true of large companies and will be dealt with later.

[9] My lovely dentist resigned after her colleague compiled a list of all the things she thought she had done wrong and sent them to the boss. This is not altogether a rare occurrence here.

as I said – he was charming and proactive. He demonstrated a more slimy and elegant version of eliminating future competition (me) and twisting the rules to his benefit. Cosying up to and palling up with the head of department is a well-known way to advance one's career and is by no means only done in Germany, and Lowlife unsurprisingly started out in this slimy vein. But he had other tricks up his sleeve. It just so happened that Useless Two was coming up to retirement. Bingo! thought Lowlife. And so he began his scheming to replace her and get himself a permanent contract. Mr Lowlife became a jack of all trades, putting his fingers in many pies as it were and making himself indispensable to the department. Almost overnight he became an expert on LGBTQ+ studies, flying here, there and everywhere to host world-changing conferences on the subject. He talked his way into getting funding so he could go off on a jolly to London with his students, all in the name of "field work".

It wasn't until my contract had ended by a few months that I learnt from a former student that Mr Lowlife had indeed got himself that permanent post he had been trying so desperately hard to obtain from the get go. I took this up with HR only to be told that his *"extraordinary qualifications"* deemed him worthy of the position. I was made somewhat curious by this wording and was eager to find out what could be more relevant for university language teaching than a PhD, so I checked out his staff profile and saw that he has an MBA. I suppose that makes him as qualified to teach English as a foreign language at a university as a sniper is qualified to work for non-violence international. But at least there's a lesson in all this: for all of you budding university instructors of English out there, make sure you get your Business Administration qualifications under your belt.

CHAPTER 6

§546 Das darfst du nicht!
You're not allowed to do that!

༄

Germany received a lot of positive press, and rightly so, for its welcoming of refugees during the refugee crisis of 2015.[10] Many Germans were compassionate and keen to help those less fortunate. That lasted for about three weeks. I would love to say that I got this kind of warm welcome when I took up a new position as an English A-level teacher in a vocational college in October of 2018. This was an important month for me, as it marked the official end of my six-year university teaching stint and the start of a new phase of working, in which I worked part-time as a salaried employee (39 per cent) and part-time as a freelancer.

On day three of the job, I needed a hole punch and found one in the opposite end of the staffroom to where my desk was located. So off I went to get it, not realising that this would constitute an infringement upon an unknown rule. As soon as I picked it up, I heard a feeble but pointed "*neeiiiinnn*" coming from a colleague in the same corner of the room. It was like a scene straight out of *Office Space*. My heart started to pound in my chest. What grave error had I just committed? Did I forget to fill out a form two months in advance asking for permission to use the object? Would I be subject to a fine of 3,000 euros for touching an object that wasn't mine even though I had no clue I couldn't touch it? All manner of scary things were racing through my mind. My colleague then went on to explain my

---

[10] Having said that, one of my German colleague's reactions to the generosity of Germans on this occasion was to ask the question, "Why do Germans have to be either really good or really bad?" I'll let you ponder this.

gross misconduct while I was standing there, palms and forehead sweating: "This hole punch can only be used by members of staff who sit in *this* corner of the staffroom." And so it was that I started to really look forward to working here and forging meaningful and lasting relationships.

"Efficient", "organised", "direct" and "thorough" are just a few of the "virtues" often thrown around when describing Germans. "*Ordnung muss sein*" (there must be order) is indeed one of Germany's favourite clichés and you hear it whenever you break an unwritten rule or don't slavishly obey bureaucrats/the state/the boss. One thing that has baffled me ever since I arrived here is a glaring inconsistency in the average German's stereotype of this "*Ordnung*". You only see it in people's interactions with the state and surroundings, but not when it comes to their interactions with each other. Take my unforgivable ten-minute lateness to school one morning. In a not altogether unusual start to the day, my tram between two towns had a technical defect meaning that I had to change trams halfway through my journey. As I always leave the house extra early to allow for these unforeseen issues, I (mistakenly) thought I'd still make it to school on time. As soon as I entered the staffroom at eight forty, I was greeted by a colleague, Herr Blockwart[11], pointing at his watch, following me to my seat and saying loud enough for everyone to hear, "Eight thirty, Ms Dunn. Lessons begin here at eight thirty."[12]

He kept up a feeble lament, like a dribbling tap which never quite gathers flow yet never quite ceases, reminding me of *ze* rules and regulations. It didn't even seem to matter that I had a free period first thing. You see, the majority of Germans love to point out other people's shortcomings and correct you for the least little mistake, since, as far as I can see, it is the expression of a need to occupy the position of "law-giver", instead of having to constantly occupy the position of passively accepting another's set of rules. It's like an involuntary tic or a really boring form of Tourette's. Moreover, their

---

[11] A *Blockwart* was the name given to a leader of a group during the rule of the Nazis.

[12] I am still on formal terms with this colleague. Strangely enough, the ice hasn't been broken yet. It is very common to address people as "Ms" or "Mr" at work and in professional settings and this can go on for years, or in some cases, forever.

reputation for "directness" seems to only apply when they believe a rule has been infringed upon, or when they are exhibiting "*Besserwisser*" (smart arse) behaviour over the most trivial of things.

At this vocational A-level college there was one other English teacher, who prior to my arrival had been the only English teacher at the college for eleven years. She wasn't best pleased when I came along to teach, and that's putting it mildly. Not only would she glare at me from her desk like she had seen me on a wanted poster, but she'd also frequently scream at me instead of talking to me and her default setting was like a bomb ready to explode, so I'll refer to her as Ms Ticking-time-bomb. She had a mixed reputation among colleagues and was the butt of several jokes among her pupils. She was involved in all things exam related at the college, such as scheduling resits, organising dates and finding invigilators. So she was useful and had some weight, which she really enjoyed throwing around. As far as her pupils were concerned, her English was abysmal. When I had to cover Ms Ticking-time-bomb's lesson on one occasion, her pupils took great delight in imitating her. "*Could you please close the Fenster?*" they would repeat to one another. Her flat, off-black knee-high boots that she wore all year round come rain, hail or shine also made a lasting impression on her pupils, culminating at the end of one school year in posters plastered around the building from her finalists, showing a pair of black boots, greying roots, and a picture of a window. The only thing missing was a bomb.

During a free period in my first fortnight at the college I went into the staffroom and even though Ms Ticking-time-bomb was the only other person there, I thought I'd try and make it look like I was working, particularly as I knew she had her eye on me. This turned out to be an unwise move. I was pretending to browse the books on the shelf and was about to pick one up when a loud, booming voice stopped me in my tracks: "*Fassen Sie die Bücher nicht an! Die sind MEINE Bücher!*" ("Don't touch the books! They're MY books!")

I pretty much froze on the spot, like a shoplifter caught in the act. It's one thing being denied the use of a hole punch I thought, but being screamed at for looking at books on a public shelf was something else entirely.

"*I* bought those books and you don't have the right to take them," she continued, only a touch more quietly than before.

Now if the books had been in a pigeonhole or labelled individually, I might have understood, but I had no idea how to deal with this outburst. The time bomb had exploded already, and all I could think about was what might set her off again, and when. While this was going through my mind, a colleague came into the staffroom and put the kettle on, and Ms Ticking-time-bomb hurried off to make a phone call. Seething, I went back to my desk and got on with some real work.

Though Ms Ticking-time-bomb had been at the college for a long time, and hence knew a thing or two about the curriculum, writing exams, policies, procedures and the like, she made it her business not to share a single useful piece of information with me. This made the entire process of designing and writing final A-level exams "*Katastophal*" with a capital "K". In this college, teachers set, mark, and grade the exams. Once the exams have been written they are sent to the city district government, checked by bureaucrats, and sent back to the school with either a "pass", "pass with revisions", or "fail and resubmit". This is where any intervention outside the college starts and finishes. Should you need to redo an exam you have a period of around two months to revise and resubmit. I was absolutely dreading preparing and writing the exams for my three courses. Everything I had done up to then I had "learnt by doing", as the Germans say. For my first draft I had no choice but to send it to Ms Ticking-time-bomb for feedback. I knew that getting constructive feedback was going to be as likely as getting free tap water at a German restaurant, but anyway, I sent off my exam questions with a whole host of other essential bumf, including an outline of my grounding, how the points are to be allocated, how all of this relates to the curriculum, and how the learning objectives, of whose existence I had been kept in the dark, had been met. My feedback consisted of the following:

You need to use roman numerals in italics instead of 1, 2 and 3. Your font is too small and the header on page 7 is incorrect.

My eye is then drawn to the text marked in bold with exclamation marks:

*And the name of the exam for your IT students is **not** 21-K-PMEDK-Ci**d**-3jITAE-1 but 21-K-PMEDK-Ci**c**-3jITAE-1!!*

The feedback, in the form of an email, finished by her stating that she was going on holiday and would be unavailable for the next three weeks. While I had been fully expecting to receive plenty of criticism, I had hoped it would be constructive in some way. I had also expected it to be related to the actual content. But not a word was said about this. It came then as no surprise to me that when the time came, all my exam proposals had to be reworked and resubmitted.

The next obstacle to surmount after my proposals had finally been accepted was the question, "to dictionary or not to dictionary?" According to the civil servants at the city district government, an English–English dictionary was allowed for my IT pupils and my business pupils, but not for my marketing and design pupils. And if that wasn't bizarre enough, there was a further snag. The director of the college suddenly realised at this point that the school didn't have any monolingual dictionaries. "How about I ask my design pupils if they can bring their own?" I ask the director, clutching at straws and hoping I can come away from this not looking like a massive fool in front of my pupils.

"Did the district government say you could do that?" came her response.

I had no desire whatsoever to contact the bureaucrats and ask them, and even if I did, time was short. A day or two passes and then the director gets back to me, as happy as Larry.

"Frau Dünn, I came across these old picture dictionaries for students of IT. They'll do nicely. You can also use them for your business class."

And so my pupils got their dictionaries in the end.

CHAPTER 7

§362 *Datenschutz über alles!*
Data protection above all else!

❧

Although dealing with these exams caused me no end of headaches and sleepless nights, it was the day-to-day snide remarks, the yelling, and attempts to show me up that really wore me down. For reasons that I have never quite understood, Germans have a particular genius when it comes to holding a grudge and investing inordinate amounts of time and energy in petty acts of revenge. When I saw that my exam feedback from my colleague consisted of nothing, I decided to speak to the director to see if she had any past papers I could consult. She told me to speak to my colleague. I told the director I had done this but to no avail. When I asked her if I could see a past paper from a few years ago which was in a drawer locked up about 2 metres away from us, she barked the by-now-typical-phrase, *"das darfst du nicht!"* ("You're not allowed to do that!") She swiftly went on to tell me that exams are locked away for data protection reasons, teachers always prepare their exams from scratch, and that's just the way it is.

Now let me just make it clear that it was never my intention to "denounce" Ms Ticking-time-bomb by speaking to the director; I merely wanted and needed assistance with exam preparation, but after this meeting with the director Ms Ticking-time-bomb came that bit closer to blowing her top once again. During a lunch break one afternoon shortly after my exchange with the director, I was rostered for fifteen minutes of "playground duty". Though it's an A-level college, every year there are always a handful of pupils under eighteen. As I sit there staring at my phone as all the pupils had left the premises, I catch a glimpse of Ms Ticking-time-bomb at the other end of the playground. She stands there glowering at me, arms crossed, not even pretending to be doing anything. After my "duty" I have a free period so I make my way to the local bakery a three-minute walk away and get myself a tea. When I return, Ms Ticking-time-bomb is still standing in the playground idly, and as soon as she sees me, she follows me so closely up to the staffroom, that I can almost hear a faint tick-tock, tick-tock, tick-tock.

I make it back to my desk unharmed whereupon I see a huge pile of papers on my desk. Wondering what fresh hell this is, I glimpse at the top few pages and see it's a syllabus, or rather syllabi. All of this was available electronically, but my colleague had an agenda. Ms Ticking-time-bomb had taken it upon herself to photocopy all three syllabi for my three courses, three years too late, and cover them in red exclamation marks and pink squiggles. It looked like an emergency timetable put together by the *Deutsche Bahn* (German Rail). Merely looking at all the shapes and lines made me nauseous.

"The director said you needed more help preparing your exams," she says loud enough for the other teachers in the staffroom to hear, including Herr Blockwart who was hovering over a new colleague's desk, "so I spent a loooong time researching and gathering information for you. I hope you'll find it useful."

Hell really hath no fury like Ms Ticking-time-bomb scorned, I thought. I picked up the papers and filed them under "r" for revenge then downloaded the information as a PDF.

Abusing that very little bit of power you have to make your colleague's life a misery was also a favourite game of King-of-the-desk in the private grammar school where I briefly taught A-level English in 2017 and had Mr Don't-tell-the-taxpayer as my boss. King-of-the-desk was the deputy headmaster. Whereas it tends to be immediately obvious in the UK who holds the position of deputy head in any given school, in Germany this tends to be something you just happen to find out over time. I often asked myself, "Who is this man who walks around with his noisy clicking shoes, tight jeans[13], huffs and puffs loudly, hangs up notices here, there and everywhere, and takes to orders from the headmaster like a pig to garbage?" As with most encounters here, my first one with

---

[13] "German fashion" is an oxymoron and deserves special treatment.

him, while I was alone in the staffroom, came with its standard share of hostility and general unpleasantness. It went something like this:

Me: putting my coat on, making it pretty clear to the perceptive observer that I'm about to leave, "See you tomorrow!"

King-of-the-desk: "You can't leave now. You need to fill in the monthly participation grades for your students."

Me: "I'm just on my way out now but I can do it tomorrow."

King-of-the-desk: No, you'll do it now! You can't just leave."

Me: "This is the first I've heard about this. I'll do it tomorrow."

King-of-the-desk: throws the form at me as I walk out of the staffroom.

The next day, looking for a little sympathy and understanding, I decided to tell a colleague about this incident. She looked at me, her eyes widened, her voice went to just above a whisper, and she slowly said, "He's our deputy head." Enough said. King-of-the-desk was to be worshipped from near and afar. If he were to ask us to get up and dance naked on the table, we would duly do so, no questions asked.

When in Germany it's worth knowing that, coupled with a love of laying down the law is a slavish obedience to rules and authority in all forms. The vocational college where I worked from 2018 to 2021 after my six-year stint at university illustrates this nicely. My colleagues here did something very unusual for teachers in Germany. They actually worked. No, seriously, they didn't take the usual school holidays, so Easter, Summer, Christmas, etc., but instead booked days off like a salaried employee of any establishment other than a school. After my first term I was so looking forward to my Easter break. When I jovially wished a colleague a nice holiday, she looked at me strangely and asked me if I'd be there next week. I told her that I thought the school would be closed for two weeks as there were no lessons.

"But you need to book your days off," she replied. She saw my confusion and added, "You work here Wednesdays and Thursdays, right? So, you have to book those two days as holidays in the non-teaching periods of the year."

Thus, in the week that followed I dutifully joined my colleagues in the staffroom for a day of reading the paper, scratching my arse, taking thirty-minute cigarette breaks, putting up new notices across the school in places difficult to find, while not answering any questions because I was too busy.

In this vocational college, unlike *any* other school or college I have come across in Germany, the teachers have a "duty" to be present thereby locking them into the staffroom during official holidays unless they book time off. Herr Blockwart loves nothing more than to secretly monitor this. Well, surely this isn't really so bad, you may be thinking. After all, this is standard procedure for thousands of employees worldwide. But it's the thinking behind this that escapes me. This is the logic part one: the vocational college is located in the same building as an institution in which the employees have compulsory presence. So, the director of the school simply thought, well, as that's the case, my teachers will also have to have compulsory presence. Frequent exchanges with my Russian colleague on the matter confirm this.

Logic part two goes like this: the college is surrounded by offices with regular 9–5 workers, who are able to peer into our windows with relative ease, and heaven forbid one sunny afternoon in early August they should witness an empty staffroom. Apparently, the sight of an empty staffroom at certain periods of the year makes the neighbouring office workers' blood boil and hence complain to the college director. How dare *they* not be working when *we* have to! What an injustice! How dare they be getting away with something we're not! *Remember – German envy.* This pettiness is a hallmark of life in Germany and has in this instance resulted in us having to have a duty of presence. My Russian friend and colleague has been the first and only member of staff to challenge this in over fifteen years. For every other teacher the German mantra stands, *"es ist halt so"* (that's just the way it is).[14]

Remember – Hermann tends to learn and implement his rules, manners included, parrot-like and seemingly without understanding them.

---

[14] It's worth learning this phrase if visiting Germany. You'll hear it all the time.

The average German over the age of forty worships authority, hierarchy and rules almost as much as money, and this authority rarely gets challenged. Those who hold a position with an iota of responsibility or who wear a uniform know how to milk it for all it's worth, secure in the knowledge that they will never be held accountable for their decisions, actions or lack thereof.

In Britain, excessive sycophancy is often ridiculed. Not here. One of my colleagues at the vocational college has the additional role of fire protection officer and just thinking about when he can impose the fire safety regulations on a sheepishly obedient audience makes him wet. He is the UK primary school equivalent of a milk monitor. The major difference being that in Germany – instead of being secretly mocked for taking pointless titles so seriously – think Gareth in Ricky Gervais's *The Office* – this gives him credibility and respect. Mr Fire Officer really went all out in our last four-hour-long conference on one of the hottest days on record. Not only did he spend a great deal of time reminding us of all the rules he'd told us a dozen times before, he also took great pride in talking about a three-part series he had started watching on German television about – you guessed it – fires. "It's just incredible how quickly these things spread." Truly a fascinating afternoon was had by all.

Whenever it comes to dealing with authority figures or mistakes made by incompetent local bureaucrats, Germans are invariably as quiet as lambs, even when they have good cause to get angry and complain. This is in stark contrast to the blunt way they speak to people on their own level, or with "*scheiß Ausländer*".[15] Hermann has dozens of manners depending on whom he is talking to. Everyone knows their place and everyone is kept in their place. With outward discipline but a strong inward grudge, Hermann accepts his standing in society. In a nutshell, Germans pick and choose who they are direct with, they're never direct with perceived superiors, and they don't like people being direct with them. I strongly believe this is one of the main reasons why customer service is so appalling in Germany. If only Germans could be as vocal and difficult here as they are with their fellow citizens, there might be more than a hope in hell they'd get more than just service with a scowl.

---

[15] "Shitty" or "bloody foreigners".

CHAPTER 8

§398 Weltmeister Kommunikation!
World champions in communication!

~~~

It is no doubt a positive thing that Germans hate other Germans as much as they hate foreigners. What boggles the mind though is the German need to discharge this hatred just as a flatulent person has to discharge gas. I'm convinced I've experienced things here that are, frankly speaking, simply not legal or at the bare minimum, stink. On the last school day of the summer term, I got called in to the director's office at the vocational college I had been working at for two years. At said college, there was either no communication or bad communication, so I knew I was in for something when I was randomly called in; I just had no idea what.

"Sit down, Ms Dunn."

I sat down and didn't have the chance to ask what the purpose of the meeting was before the director barked, "I've noticed you're often sick and frequently come to work late. I wonder why this is."

I asked her to elaborate, as, bar my once ten-minute lateness, my approximate three phone calls in three years to warn her that my tram hadn't come so I may be late (and then having arrived on time), and having spent the day before this meeting at home doubled up with period pain, I was at a loss as to how to understand this bold accusation.

"Could you give me some concrete examples?" I asked. "It's true," I went on, "that I have had to call you before to say I might be late. But then I arrived on time after all."

"You're a part-time member of staff who only works two days a week so it's very obvious when you're not here," the director snapped, her face getting redder with every word.

As I was in such a state of shock, I wasn't really able to fight my corner. I remained silent, racking my brains for some sort of explanation for this. Then I suddenly remembered something that might be pertinent. "Are you referring to that time when I collapsed on my way to work and called the secretary to say I was feeling unwell and couldn't come in?"

"I wasn't thinking of that particular occasion, Ms Dunn."

"Do you have a list or note of the dates when I wasn't in?" I asked her.

"Not on me; I'll have to dig them out," she was quick to add, before changing the topic. "Due to the Covid pandemic we're going to have to reduce your hours next term," was her next statement.

"I'm sorry?"

"It's not just you," she hastened to add. "Our pupil intake for next year is much lower than expected and several members of staff will have fewer classes. In fact, staff here are used to fluctuations in class numbers and sizes. Please go to the owner's office straight away and sign your new contract with him."

I never did sign that new contract, not after being spoken to like that. The next year with the smaller intake of pupils was my final year at the vocational college. It was again characterised by the usual poor communication and reprimands, and not always petty, though taken up a notch. Ms Ticking-time-bomb also happened to be head of examinations and she took great pleasure in rostering me in for an up-until-then unheard-of position. I was to be "toilet monitor". And I wasn't asked; I was told. During the final exams it was my duty to sit in the corridor and check that when pupils left the exam to go to the toilet, they didn't switch floors. This was because if they switched floors they could cheat, whereas if they went to the toilet on the same floor, they couldn't. My colleague was frequently close by and ready to yell at me in front of pupils if I happened to be sitting in the wrong part of the corridor at the wrong time. Every so often a member of staff happened to walk by, see me sitting in an empty corridor and ask what on earth I was doing there. "But we've never done this before," was the only explanation I got.

After my pretty dismal accounts of working life in Germany, should you be interested in finding out a bit more about what it's like to work not just in schools, but in any company, why not look up the website *Kununu,* where employees can anonymously review their employers? Just for fun, you can count the number of times you see the words *"hierarchy", "mobbing"* (the German word for bullying), terrible *"Kommunikation", "Angst",* and *"kein Teamwork".* In her very recent study, Ilse Wehrmann, who writes about the collapse of early education in Germany, mentions the atmosphere of bullying, control, and fear that many teachers are subjected to. She quotes a teacher, Max, who says that he sometimes feels like he is "in the Stasi interrogation room".[16] The parallels with Herr Blockwart are striking.

Sitting all on my lonesome while watching the odd pupil leave the classroom in order to relieve themself was when it dawned on me once and for all that I had no future there. Sure, there had been several warning signs before this – the abysmal communication, the petty reprimands from my colleagues, the complete lack of social interaction, the absence of information needed for me to do my job – but this was the icing on the cake. In spite of the strength of my convictions, however, I felt a strong sense of duty towards my pupils. After all, I had a good relationship with them, and one thing my director conveniently forgot in all those ghastly meetings was the time she told me, with a great sense of surprise, that not one pupil had ever made a complaint against me. And that this was practically unheard of. Indeed, I had grown very fond of my three classes and this was strengthened when I once started a lesson fighting back tears as I had just discovered someone I knew (albeit not very well) had recently passed away. Even though I managed not to cry when I told them what I had just discovered, I was visibly shaken. One boy then came up to me saying he needed a sheet of paper and when he got to my desk, he discreetly handed me a tissue. That lesson then went like a dream. We did group work and finished with a short presentation where they had to sell Germany to the British. There were lots of sausages, beer and laughter. What I learnt was that these young eighteen- and nineteen-year-olds were actually very mature and empathetic underneath it all; I just didn't have the opportunity to see this

---

[16] *Der Kita-Kollaps: Warum Deutschland endlich auf frühe Bildung setzen muss!,* Ilse Wehrmann, Herder, 2023, p. 94.

before. I didn't need to feel any shame for being momentarily upset at the start of class, and my being open with my pupils and treating them like adults made them open up to me in return.

A pupil approached me shortly after this lesson and apologised for not showing an interest in English. She had been humiliated by her previous English teacher so understandably didn't feel comfortable in my classroom. She mentioned how she was always picked on to read aloud in class and then mocked by the teacher for her pronunciation errors. Though I couldn't change what had happened in her previous school, I did my best to make her feel welcome and valued in my class, and over time she started participating. This is not the only time I felt I had bonded and made a connection with my pupils, so I held on to this to remind myself of why I had decided to become a teacher in the first place, and that's how I resolved to stick it out for a further year.

Year three was when I was faced with the task of writing the final examinations for my three classes. As you know I had no assistance from the college whatsoever. Luckily a former university student of mine who had since completed his teacher training, the German "*Staatsexamen*" sat with me in a Zoom meeting for over two hours and went through my exams with a fine-tooth comb, giving me heaps of information which I really could have done with much earlier. On top of this, he wouldn't take a penny for his services. You see, all three of my exam proposals had been rejected by the city district government. I was fully expecting this to happen; colleagues had told me that exams are never accepted by first-time teachers and it's not uncommon for more experienced teachers to have their exams rejected, too, including Herr Blockwart. So I was all the more shocked when, once again, at the end of the working day I was called into the director's office.

"Ms Dunn, I find it strange that all your exams were rejected," was my greeting.

"I did my best with what little information I had," I answered. Somewhat emboldened by previous meetings of this kind, I went on, "And do you remember me telling you that my colleague refused to share materials with me and that I asked to see past exams but you wouldn't let me for data protection reasons?"

"Past exams are locked away and we can't access them," she responded.

I said nothing.

"Ms Dunn, your exam rejections put the school in a bad light. We simply cannot let you show the school up like this."

In hindsight I should have pointed out that I wasn't the only teacher to have had exams rejected. But that's the beauty of hindsight. In the heat of the moment, I was incapable of uttering a single word in response. Being on fairly good terms with the director's boss and owner of the college, I told him about my experiences one afternoon. Fast-forward a few months and I write them a letter of resignation. Being the decent sort of guy he is, he asked me to come and see him for a chat before leaving the college (formal exit interviews are not common in Germany). I didn't need much time to prepare for this meeting as everything was so fresh in my mind. I also had it on good authority that the owner was on bad terms with the director and he wanted rid of her. Which is why when I went to his office and saw his two assistants plus an employment lawyer, I was, at least this time, mentally prepared for a difficult discussion. Having to engage the services of an employment lawyer has been par for the course for me so far here (remember the university where a colleague somehow got a permanent position on her two-year contract, for example?), so this time I was as cool as a cucumber.

Große-Kock and Muffgold

At the vocational college, the lawyer, a member of the firm *Winter und Große-Kock,* was competent, clear and sympathetic towards my woes; fortunately, his behaviour didn't live up to his name. Shortly after our meeting I learnt that the director had resigned but hadn't told anyone. It turned out that my meeting with the lawyer was more about developing grounds to fire the director than anything else, but I had no qualms about that. What's more, the director really chose her moment to break the good news. On 1 July 2021, the day of the school leaving ceremony and the first real get-together during the pandemic with pupils excited to be getting their A-level certificates and moving on with their lives, the director decides to tell us that this is her last day at the school, too. At the end of the formal ceremony, after the pupils had received their certificates and just before the director dropped her bombshell, I heard someone faintly whispering to me what I believed was my name: "Ebigil. Psst. Ebigil."

I turned round and saw a colleague, the one who wouldn't let me use his hole punch, beckon me over.

"Ebigil, can you help get the beer and snacks ready? We're a little short on staff but we need everything ready for when the pupils come out of the hall."

Another stunning example of planning I say to myself. "Sure," I replied. "Where is everything?" As we had decided against having a communal kitchen, I wasn't sure where the goods were.

"Up in the staffroom. Where else?"

So up I went upstairs. Lo and behold at a table next to the bookcase was a whole array of beer and goodies staring me in the face. I think I must have just assumed when I came in that morning that they were for the staff who sat in that corner of the room only. When I step a little closer to the table, an interesting label stares back at me, "*Muffgold*". Once I finish laughing to myself, I remember that there is a suburb close to where I live called Muffendorf, and it transpires they have their own beer. All that glitters in this college certainly isn't gold, I thought to myself.

Everything goes according to the lack of plan and within no time, staff and pupils alike are feeling slightly merry. I even got a little tipsy on that delicious *Muffgold*. Picture the scene: youngsters celebrating for what must have been the first time in a year of pandemic, pupils and teachers drinking champagne together, exchanging meaningful and slightly drunken words, balloons bouncing around the hall, and then, suddenly, the director calls *all* her staff inside for a meeting. My colleagues exchange worried glances and we quickly gather in the hall. Inside the silence is deadly and you could cut the atmosphere with one of the knives we'd just used to cut cake. Against a backdrop of singing and dancing pupils outside, the director proceeds to tell us, in between sniffles, that she will no longer be with us. Mr Fire Officer punches the wall and screams out "*Pisser!*" ("Mother*****/a***hole!"); Herr Blockwart skulks around in the background, hands in pockets, head down; and Ms Ticking-time-bomb stomps out of the room slamming the door behind her. Nothing but a good old bit of German theatrics where heartfelt and genuine emotion would have done the job nicely. Once this sophisticated display of emotion passes, a few colleagues go up to hug the director and I decide to make my way home. I'd had more than enough excitement for one day, largely but not solely owing to that killer combination of *Muffgold* and *Kock*.

CHAPTER 9

§251 Deutsche Gründlichkeit!
German Rigour!

ᗡᗢᗣ

Turning my back for good on the vocational college and making my way into a new job, a university of applied sciences, on a 100 per cent freelance basis, seemed like a pleasant way to start afresh and put all the college dramas behind me. But prior to this I had never worked solely as a freelancer in Germany and once again, I was in for a nasty shock. To paraphrase Stephen Clarke, I'd already been through purgatory so I figured I might as well go the whole way and see what hell had to offer. I was excited about taking up this post; a headhunter who works for the university had given me a heads-up about an opening for a permanent position, and she was really keen for me to apply.

In the "efficient" land of Hermann, getting your invoices paid takes an awful lot of time, patience, and determination. The thing is, the basic concept really wasn't that hard – fill in an invoice from the university admin department, submit it and wait for the money to appear in your bank account. In the eight months that I worked there not once was I paid on time. January's pay, for example, arrived in mid-April. This university of applied sciences expects its freelancers to have Adobe Acrobat Pro DC installed on their computers without telling them so. Because everyone has this expensive version, right? Only this particular type of form is compatible with the university's system and only this type of form will make it possible to complete invoices correctly, as I found out several months into my job. When I fill in their invoice my income always comes out in millions. The invoice, which *they* provided me with and which *they* insist I use, will not let me change this. In

November, a civil servant from the admin department calls me to tell me how we can resolve this:

> Civil servant: "Your earnings are coming out in the millions. We cannot accept that."
>
> Me: "Yes. I understand. The form will not let me edit the amount."
>
> Civil servant: "This has never happened before. How strange."[17]
>
> Silence.
>
> Me: "What can I do? Do you have a new form I can use perhaps?"

After a few more awkward silences, a bit of being told off and put in my place, the civil servant comes up with what appears to be a practical solution. Hurrah!

> Civil servant: "This is what we'll do from now on. Write out the following sentence in every email, *'according to the invoice, I have earned X. However, the real amount is X.'*"

I proceed in this way and for the months of October and November I am lucky enough to get paid with only a shortish delay of around a month. But then in December the rules suddenly and without warning change. I find out that my civil servant friend has since retired and now all hell breaks loose; our "plan" is shattered to smithereens. Several emails are once again sent telling me to change the final sum in the invoice as it's in the millions and that's not correct. Several answers are sent by me repeating the same information that their forms won't let me do this. On 16 February I finally get paid for December. Result! But I cannot receive my pay for January. Because, in true German fashion, things must be overly complicated, systems which work must be changed, and the person on the receiving end of this must be the last to find out. Now, in order

---

[17] When things don't work or someone hasn't done what they ought to have done, it's either "*komisch*" (strange) or the slightly less frequent "*doof*" (silly).

to get paid for January I need to print out my invoice, cross out the sum in the millions and write the correct sum in pen, scan it and email it back to the university. Having left my scanner in 1992 and not being a paid employee of the university administration, I'm obviously unable to proceed in this way.

But that's not where the fun and games end. For March there is a *new* issue with my invoice. Now the problem is that I have apparently selected the wrong tax option from their drop-down menu. When I ask why my previous invoices were accepted if the tax information I selected was wrong, I'm just told, with the usual amounts of huffing and puffing, that they shouldn't have been accepted. Rather than be helpful and openly tell me which option to choose, I am told that I should contact a tax advisor if I have any questions. A tax advisor that could typically cost around 250 euros an hour, that is. I then remember, when I've finished fuming, that a former student of mine teaches Italian to a lawyer. My student understands my predicament and wishes to help me, so he gives me the contact details of his lawyer student (not *Große-Kock)* and I email him a chain of communication between me and the university. The lawyer contacts the university, works his magic, and suddenly they are only too happy to sort out my payment. Many Germans, you see, are all huff, puff, bluster and handbags at ten paces but if you really muster up enough courage and get in their face, they will wilt faster than a hydrangea in the Sahara. For the month of April, I get paid promptly like a regular human being and naively believe the issue has thus been dealt with.

Even though all my jobs here to date have entailed multiple almighty cock-ups, I have been equally sad to leave them as the interaction with the students and pupils has always been so rewarding. I'll never forget our first lesson "in person" around April 2022. I was sitting in an empty classroom with a broken overhead projector on the floor with tape wrapped around it (to make it extremely clear it wasn't working), thereby feeling reassured that nothing had changed at universities since before the pandemic. I was waiting with some trepidation for my students to arrive; we'd never met in person before. Soon I start hearing voices and laughter and my students appear in a large group all together and make their way to their seats. They seemed so genuinely happy and excited to be back in a classroom you'd have thought they were going out clubbing. During our thirty-minute break outside they ask me to join them and we have a nice chat about all sorts, and back in the classroom the group work on British politics is entertaining and eye-opening; one student came across that famous photo of Ed Miliband eating a bacon sandwich and with it provoked a lot of laughs in the classroom.

So once again I find myself battling with mixed feelings. On the one hand, I realise that all this bureaucratic chaos and terrible communication is taking its toll on me, not to mention the long periods without pay. I start to wonder how I'm going to write the exams without assistance, how much unpaid time I'll have to spend on them, how I'll grade them and whether a marking scheme is even available, and most importantly, whether the job might lead to a permanent position as I was told at interview. As I mentioned, even *before* I was interviewed, I had been headhunted for a permanent post. When I started the job, the headhunter again reminded me to apply and to let her know as soon as I had submitted my application any time before 30 January. That date rolls around and I don't hesitate to let her know that I've sent my application. When it came to the end of April and I heard no more about the permanent position, I started to panic again. This caused no end of sleepless nights. Yet on the other hand, I had built up a strong relationship with my students, working with them was so easy and stress-free. It was an all-too-familiar dilemma for me by now. Should I put up with the catastrophic working conditions, lack of respect and pay so that I can continue to carry out enjoyable work with great people, or should I not tolerate the toxic work environment but potentially screw over my students by quitting?

After very careful consideration and an extremely frank and moving discussion with my students, I decided to end my contract prematurely. The possibility of a permanent position turned out to be nothing other than a carrot waved in front of my face so that the university could hire a member of staff very cheaply (paid hourly) as a stop-gap. This was presumably as they didn't have the funds to create a full position in 2021–22 (at least this is what I experienced at my first university). While browsing an English teacher's and colleague's blog I discovered that interviews for the permanent position had since begun, and I hadn't heard a dicky bird. Was it because I was vocal about my problems with pay that they didn't contact me, or was it down to the fact that I was just a handy means for them to cheaply find someone at the last minute and they never considered me for the permanent post in the first place? Well, I'll never know. All I knew was that I'd had enough of being mistreated. As my students were the ones who had kept me going, I decided to open up to them one lesson and let them know everything I had experienced and why it was, therefore, pretty much impossible to continue until the end of the semester.

I wasn't looking forward to this and had expected to be met with quite a bit of confrontation and anger. After all, the students had done nothing wrong and here was their instructor saying she was seriously thinking about leaving shortly before their exams; my timing wasn't exactly great. What I actually experienced once again showed me how fortunate I had been to teach such compassionate and understanding young adults. For the first time ever, all eighteen cameras were switched on in Zoom for the entire duration of our meeting. I shared with them my manifold problems, told them that it was getting really tough for me to continue paying my quarterly tax instalments *in advance* when my pay was so erratic. Against expectations they understood and even supported my decision to leave, but they didn't want me to. They asked me if, to my mind, this was a one-off problem, or whether it reflected some deep-seated structural issue. They dug deeply and really wanted to get to the bottom of it. One student, who had a small child with complex health issues and, I therefore assume, better things to do than help sort out this mess, wasted no time and called the head of department immediately after class to see if some compromise could be met. My student confronted the head about my pay issues, asked if they could speed up my outstanding pay for May and pay me a token fee for the writing and marking of examinations over the summer.

While the department was busy umming and ahing I received warm messages of sympathy from several students, including one big thank you from a young man as I had introduced him to Kim Wilde in our English pop lesson! Eventually I heard from the head of department but her offer and tone left a lot to be desired. Alas with a very heavy heart I left the university of applied sciences. Naturally I felt very guilty, but a student wrote to me shortly after to say that the class continued to support my decision, and what's more, their exams were really easy in the end.

CHAPTER 10

§742 Weltmeister Planung!
World champion planners!

৹৵৵৹

Even though I was by no means rolling in money, I decided to take a holiday in July following my ordeal at the university of applied sciences. I was really looking forward to spending two weeks in the French countryside. As all freelancers know, however, I couldn't take a complete break from teaching as the prospect of earning nothing was just too dismal. So shortly before going away I got in touch with a language school which, to my surprise, just happened to be looking for an English teacher as their permanent and contracted teacher of English had recently left. My timing for once seemed too good to be true. I had given some lessons there, during the approximately two-and-a-half-months' university semester break, back in 2014 and the director, also known as Ms String-along, recognised me and seemed happy to throw work my way right from the start. Her enthusiasm was contagious. "I can give you twenty, thirty hours a week. Just say the word." As I was just about to go on holiday, we agreed that we would start slowly with around five hours of online teaching a week. I didn't want to spend my whole holiday working after all. Then we would build up gradually and finally agree upon a fixed number of hours per week.

Though the language school frequently bombarded me with phone calls while I was trying to switch off from it all with cider and apple tarts, I politely and patiently dealt with last-minute schedule changes and the like as I really wanted to build up to twenty hours of teaching and make a positive impression. When I returned to Germany my hours started to increase as discussed and there was an additional treat in store: I could be given a contracted job as a salaried employee. Here's how this works: a lady close to retirement age had taken the contracted position from the English teacher who had recently left. Soon after she took up the position, however, she became ill and was unable to work. Ms String-along said that I could have that contracted position, of which there is one per subject. The contract would be ready by September. Fast-forward to September and the contract is not ready. Not to worry, Ms String-along assures me, it will be ready by November. November comes around and guess what happens? Is there a contract? Of course there isn't. Naturally I start to have serious doubts at this stage, but I also need to think about things like being able to pay bills, insurances and tax instalments. It's now settled that the contract will be available in January. All that remains is a chat about the terms and conditions.

As thirty hours seemed somewhat ambitious, what with my other teaching assignments, we settled on twenty. Ms String-along actively encouraged me not to give up my other freelance engagements, which was considerate but slightly concerning. Not so positive was the news that I would have twenty days' paid holiday per year, rather than the more typical thirty days. Additionally, I wanted to make sure that, as is customary, I would receive a higher wage for courses in specialised and technical English. So far, I had been paid the same hourly rate for general conversation courses and courses with mechanical engineers. A week or so later I went back to the school and we had another chat where I expressed my disappointment with the twenty days' holiday. Ms String-along agreed we could make it twenty-four days. She also assured me that I would be paid more for technical courses. I left this informal meeting feeling proud that I had managed to argue my corner and was looking forward to getting the contract in my hands.

The contract materialised on 30 January, 2023, when I had given up hope and had started to cut my losses. On this Monday, a day where I have ten hours of teaching as Ms String-along knows all too well, I was once again bombarded with phone calls asking for my date of birth, my tax band, the name of my health insurance provider, and my social security number. Heaven only knows why it had taken the school this long to ask for such crucial information. For the sake of finally getting a contract and hence a bit of financial security, I dealt with the multiple requests between classes and arranged to go and sign the contract later that week.

At the start of February, I'm back at the language school to review the contract. Alarm bells start to ring immediately. I check the clause about holiday entitlement, and "twenty days" stares back at me. I look for the clause about salary to verify that I'll be paid more for my specialised courses, but there is no such clause. It's really like an extremely frustrating game of hide and seek. Then comes the real kick in the teeth. A line has been crossed through the clause which stipulates how many hours I'll be working per week. Annoyed but not really surprised any more, I decide to try and tackle the issues one by one:

Me: "I see here that there are twenty days' holiday per year. I thought we agreed on twenty-four."

Ms String-along: "If I give you twenty-four days then that's unfair towards the other two salaried teachers who have twenty days' holiday."

Me: "So that means we can't be flexible? It is twenty days or nothing?"

Ms String-along: "I can give you unpaid holiday time whenever you want. You'll find that no other schools are this accommodating."

Me: "There is a line through the clause which stipulates my working hours. Didn't we agree on twenty?"

Ms String-along: "Yes, but you recently gave up a course with those mechanical engineers in Berlin, and the Friday morning course with Colliers is currently on a break."

Me: "I really don't mind if there are fewer hours in the contract, say sixteen, as what I'm interested in is having the security I didn't have as a freelancer."

I really want to have as a minimum a set number of hours and I spend a fair amount of time talking about the importance of financial security. She knows this is important to me after I told her about my ordeals with previous jobs, yet getting a straight answer from her is like trying to nail jelly to a wall. No sooner have I begun my plea for fixed hours than she goes off on a tangent telling me about her recent crisis involving her school, Google, ambiguous search entries, a lawyer and a £5,000 fine she has to pay as soon as possible. She's talking at record speed, getting very emotional, and I'm struggling to keep up. I try to find a way back to the topic but she gets there first.

> Ms String-along: "The thing is, in the upcoming months of May and June there are lots of public holidays on Thursdays, and many companies take the Friday off as well as a bridge day."
>
> Me: "Well what about after the summer? Wha—?"
>
> Ms String-along (cutting me off): "And it's not advantageous for you if you agree to sixteen hours rather than twenty because then I have to give you less holiday pay. You'll be paid for sixteen hours rather than twenty. You'll lose out."
>
> Me: "Speaking of holiday, if there is no fixed number of weekly hours in my contract, how will you work out my weekly holiday pay?"
>
> Ms String-along: I'll base it on the week or weeks leading up to your holiday. But I want to be fair nonetheless. It wouldn't be right if you had a week with lots of cancellations and let's say, just ten hours. I'd have to balance it out with previous weeks. But we can cross that bridge when we come to it."
>
> Me: "Wouldn't it just be less hassle to put in a fixed number of hours as agreed instead of leaving it at zero hours as it currently stands? The security is really important to me."
>
> Ms String-along: "Then I'd need to speak to my advisor."

A week later I hand in my resignation. But before doing so, I have another heart-to-heart with my students, just like I did at the university of applied sciences. Over the last years and against my will I'd become a bit of an expert at telling students why I couldn't teach them any more, so I wasn't feeling particularly daunted by this prospect. Over Zoom I summarise my problems with the language school, trying to strike a balance between being frank and professional – a bit of a tightrope walk. I start off with my C1/C2 class. Once again, my students are extremely sympathetic. Two in the group suggest that I come and work for them independently, telling me they have been messed about in the past by the language school, they're tired of the high staff turnover rate, and, most importantly, they enjoy my lessons and for the first time feel they are doing something challenging; apparently C2 courses are not easy to find. Over the next few weeks, they try to sort something out. They send me emails, we meet for coffee and updates, but they're unfortunately tied to the language school for at least another year. Too many obstacles are in the way but I am touched by the proposal and resolve to keep in touch. Who knows? Maybe I'll have the privilege to work with them again one day in the not-too-distant future.

Only in Germany: *Wieso einfach wenn's auch kompliziert geht?*

What makes freelancing even more difficult here is that it's all too easy to fall into the trap of "*Scheinselbstständigkeit*", which translates as "bogus" or "pseudo-self-employment". Pseudo-self-employment is the term for an employment relationship in which a contractor/ freelancer contractually titled as self-employed is an employee according to objective criteria and would have to be registered as such subject to compulsory insurance. I'm sure that this would also be problematic in the UK, but perhaps the rules and regulations are slightly easier to navigate there than in Hermann's world. Up until 2019, it was quite easy to find out if you were pseudo-self-employed, as the law stipulated quite clearly that you could not spend more than three-quarters or 75 per cent of your time working for one sole employer. If you spent more than 75 per cent of your time with one employer then you were entitled to a contract. Since 2019, however, good old Germany has decided that this regulation wasn't complicated enough, so they spruced it up a bit. After all, why have a law that's easy to understand and adhere to? Why make it simple when it can be complicated, or, as the Germans say, "*wieso einfach wenn's auch kompliziert geht?*" Now you need to spend five-sixths of your time with one employer (83.3 per cent!) before you can have the right to a contract. This not only strikes me as a random figure plucked out of thin air, hence a law which is all too easy to accidently break, but also a nice way to screw freelancers. I mean, how likely is it that a freelancer will get so much work from one sole employer, or that they will even *know* that this very random and precise amount of their working time is with only one employer? "*Das kann nicht wahr sein*", "that can't be true", as Hermann would say.

CHAPTER 11

§319 *Ich bin ehrlich und ich sage meine Meinung*

I'm direct and say what's on my mind

❧

Germans pride themselves on being "direct", "honest" and "to the point", and they're often more than happy to highlight this whether it's relevant or not. I've recently been on the receiving end of this German "directness" for a petty and banal matter myself. My relationship with my landlady, henceforth to be referred to as Hyacinth Bucket – comically pronounced 'Bouquet' – from the wonderful sitcom *Keeping Up Appearances* due to her, well, need to keep up appearances, severely deteriorated over the last year or so of my tenancy. I lived in the same house as her, in a granny flat, though had a separate entrance and living quarters. She and her family were very partial to being loud after 10 p.m., which is outside the official hours where you are legally allowed to make noise.

German law stipulates that the hours between 10 p.m. and 6 a.m., sometimes 7 a.m., are "quiet hours" and this extends to Sunday afternoons, where one is generally not allowed to wash one's car, put bottles into a bottle bank, mow the lawn, and be loud and disrespectful. Now very few people adhere to this admittedly, but at least there is a law to fall back on should you need it. After weeks of waking up in the middle of the night with feelings of a slight heart attack to the sound of elephants stomping above me, the washing machine on its final spin, men yelling at each other from one room to the next, I decided to politely confront Mrs Bucket via text message about the noise and the effect it was taking on my health. The response I got was that "boys will be boys". Well, you can imagine my relief upon hearing that the issue had thus been dealt with accordingly. Of course, things didn't stop there.

The peak of my noise disturbance had been planned well in advance in the Bucket residence. "Abigail, I'm glad I bumped into you," said Mrs Bucket as I was making my way out the flat one morning. "It's my son's twenty-first birthday later this week and on Thursday he's having his friends over for a party." She was looking at me intently, trying her best to read my expression without managing to be discreet about it. "It won't be quiet," she continued. "My husband and I have arranged to stay at a friend's so that my son can have the house to himself."

"Oh," I stammered.

"I'm sorry I didn't tell you earlier; I kept meaning to but then I kept forgetting. You know how it is. Do you perhaps have a friend you can stay with?"

I didn't have to think too hard as no one came to mind who a) had a spare bed or sofa, b) could put me up at such short notice, and c) could do it on a week night. But at least this way of informing me was much more open and honest than the time she just had to drop into conversation that her son was handing in his bachelor's thesis one Wednesday in July; her way of informing me that there would be a party to celebrate that night.

"I'll sort something out," I said to her.

In truth, the only thing I could do was get a hotel room for the night. I consoled myself with the thought that I'd always wondered what it'd be like to stay in a hotel in my own town. So I booked a room in the city centre, brought my favourite book and a big bar of Lindt raspberry chocolate, and resolved to make the most of it.

The day after the spontaneous hotel stay, I had my three-year check-up at my GP's, who had his practice on my street. So, on Friday morning, just after the rush-hour traffic I embarked on the twenty-minute bus journey back to mine and the doctor's. All was going fine and dandy until the bus driver suddenly stopped, unable to turn a corner. The reason? A "*Falschparker*", "parking offender" had parked his Mercedes in a curve. I looked at my watch. "If this doesn't sort itself out soon, I'm going to miss my appointment," I keep saying to myself. This is where my "*Kopfkino*", "mental cinema", starts to kick in. I imagine all sorts of scenarios; missing my appointment and having to wait an eternity for the next one, being scolded by the receptionist for being late, and then – horror of horrors – explaining the reason for my lateness when I live on the same road as the practice! The situation soon resolves itself as the driver finally manages, albeit it at a snail's pace, to get his bus around the corner without hitting the shiny Mercedes. I arrive at the doctor's just a few minutes late but very flustered. The first thing that happens is my blood pressure is taken.

"Frau Dünn, your pressure's quite high which concerns me as you're a small and slim woman," the doctor says, not-so-reassuringly.

Not wanting to take any risks, and not taking into account the fact that I arrived slightly out of breath and panicked, the doctor tells me I am to wear a Holter monitor to record my pressure over a period of twenty-four hours, including when I'm in bed. And we're not talking about a small, compact device here. This was something you had to sling over yourself akin to wearing a bulky handbag.

"The machine will beep every fifteen minutes when it takes a reading. Don't let this bother you," says my GP.

My *Kopfkino* goes into overdrive. What if I'm already suffering from high blood pressure and I'm barely forty? How can I stay calm with this device strapped to my body, especially when I have the cast of Riverdance living above me? Will I become a problem patient for the German health insurance? With all sorts of thoughts flooding my mind I make my way to the receptionist to pick up the monitor.

"It's out on loan today and tomorrow. Come back in a few days," she barks.

"I see. Should I make an appointment?"

"No, just come back in two days. We'll reserve the monitor for you."

It's nothing short of a miracle that my blood pressure readings eventually came back fine. I took this all as a sign to not get so wound up so quickly and to pay more attention to my health, but as always, it was much easier said than done, especially when embroiled in disputes with your landlady.

When Mrs Bucket's, sorry Mrs Bouquet's, daughter was getting ready for her wedding[18] all manner of noise took over the house once more. Prior to this it wasn't infrequent for the family to do somewhere between 100 laps up and down the house in between flushing the toilet constantly. This went on well into the early hours when the wedding was being prepared for. (I'm still not sure to this day what they were doing. The wedding and reception were taking place in a castle after all.) My text messages to Mrs Bouquet got more frequent and aggressive in tone, and yes, I did, in the throes of sleep deprivation and stress, threaten to call the "*Ordnungsamt*"[19] if I kept on losing sleep. I felt really awkward bumping into her after my not-so-friendly texts and I imagined she'd raise the topic of *Ordnungsamt*, but she never did. Instead, she repeatedly asked me to go out and enjoy my terrace in this lovely spell of weather instead of sitting indoors. Now it's true that I don't have the greenest of fingers and I had been neglecting my terrace. The little table was largely covered in bird crap and my big candle had melted and looked like a wrinkly, oversized penis (it didn't help that it was the colour of flesh). Very quickly Mrs Bouquet's demands soon started to get a little more pointed, however. When I have a spare moment, I might like to sweep up the leaves and clean up my table, she frequently remarked. It soon became clear that her comments were falling upon deaf ears so she quite literally decided to take matters into her own hands and fix my table herself. "There," she said, "I've made it all nice and new for you."

"Oh," I said, as it seemed the most appropriate response.

I was coming home from work one evening a few days later just minding my own business when I saw a bunch of tables and chairs being put out in front of my landlady's house and in her garden. This, I was to learn, was all in aid of the drinks reception to take place the evening before the wedding. And so, the penny dropped. I couldn't possibly let the side down with my manky garden equipment, could

---

[18] This was her second wedding. Two weddings are typical in Germany. It's common to have the first wedding towards the end of the calendar year to save a massive amount of tax. Then you can have your second wedding, preferably in summer and not in a church, because then you could be liable to pay church tax.

[19] The "Office for Public Order" (nice Orwellian touch to it, don't you think?) has no direct equivalent in England. The most similar institution would probably be Environmental Health.

I? What on earth would the wedding guests think? Although a valuable lesson had been learnt about the importance of cultivating appearances, I didn't know what to make of the much-reputed German "directness". Why couldn't Mrs Bouquet have just mentioned that she was having guests round for an evening? I didn't need to reflect on this issue of directness for much longer though, as soon after I began to get requests from her to meet up for a chat. After about the fourth request consisting of exactly the same message – do I have fifteen minutes for a chat? – I decided to bite the bullet and actually try to find out what exactly the purpose of this chat was.[20]

"It's about our relationship and the way in which it has changed," was the answer. As it was March 2020 and the Covid pandemic was wreaking havoc in my daily life, I told Mrs Bouquet I would be available to meet the following week, once I had managed to get my online teaching off the ground and a bit more stability back in my life. But my setting the terms and conditions of this chat was a big no-no. Mrs Bouquet didn't take too kindly to having to wait, and a day later she cornered me outside my front door as I was coming back from a walk only to tell me that she had decided to give me my notice. Again, I wasn't too sure about the link between "relationship" and "getting rid of me", but that, it seems, is the result of me standing up for myself and calling her out on her behaviour, namely the constant noise. *Remember – an offended German is like a hand grenade.* Though people frequently praise Germany for its solid system of tenant's rights (it's true that landlords are often stuck with undesirable tenants), this did not apply to me as I inhabited what's known as a granny flat. I can therefore be given notice not only without a valid legal reason, but without any reason whatsoever.

It goes without saying that the months following this were anything but happy. Secure in the knowledge that there were no longer consequences of actions to be feared, the Bouquet residence really went to town on the noise front. One night at 11 p.m. I heard the family singing "Happy Birthday" (it had to be 11 p.m. on the dot as my landlady was born at 11 p.m. I later found out). I knew what this meant – another improvised party had just started and would go

---

[20] In Germany important information is often withheld from you for as long as possible. Instead, it's given to you in little dribs and drabs, but never all at once.

on till the early hours. So out came my violin. Now I'd been having violin lessons for around two-and-a-half years at this point and as much as I love the instrument, I never once imagined that my greatest joy would be playing to an audience of anywhere between two and five living above me. But I had at least moved up in the music world though. Prior to this I would bounce a plastic measuring jug off the floor. Honestly, I thoroughly recommend this as a way of getting revenge on noise. The shrill sound of the jug bouncing off the floor was painful even for me so I could only imagine what it was doing for them. Not being the best of cooks, I never actually used the jug for its original purpose, but I was delighted to have found a use for it in this way.

CHAPTER 12

§814 *"Vorsprung durch Technik"*

∽∾∿

One day in 2016 something really strange and frightening happened to me. I woke up with the crazy idea of going on a spontaneous train trip with a good friend of mine. "Train" is perhaps better referred to in Germany as "chariot of doom". After arriving at the station slightly later than planned, and somewhat out of breath, my friend finds an employee of the *Deutsche Bahn* and proceeds to ask them if the train on the platform right behind us goes to Frankfurt. (If you've ever had the misfortune to experience *Deutsche Bahn*, you'll know that getting from A to B requires the same level of skill and general absurdity needed to complete a round of *Takeshi's Castle*.) The bureaucrat replies that it does not, without turning around to even so much as glance at the platform, and adds no further information. A couple of minutes later, I hear a whistle and see the doors closing of a train on the platform opposite; I continue to watch as it slowly pulls out of the station. We then realise that that train also goes to Frankfurt, but it's a regional train and not an inter-city one. Why did the German Rail employee not tell us this, you surely wonder? Because my friend didn't ask about *that specific* train. The *Deutsche Bahn* employee did not draw the obvious corollary, being that I am asking about a train to Frankfurt because ultimately, I wish to go to Frankfurt.

The way I see it, in Germany you must remember to ask *exact* questions as if you were getting three wishes from an extremely hostile genie. The higher the person is up the chain, the more precise and exact these questions need to be. By way of example, if you ask whether a train goes from say, Berlin to Cologne, and the reply is yes, this is not enough. You must also ascertain that it does not go to Cologne via London or Dubrovnik. Not long after arriving in my new home town I wandered down to the bus station to enquire about getting a monthly pass. The exchange I had with the customer service representative behind the desk was most helpful indeed (spoiler alert: you'll need stronger than usual intellectual capacities to keep up with this one):

> Me: "Hello. I've just arrived in the city and I need to buy a monthly ticket. What are my options?"
>
> Customer service representative: "There are various kinds of tickets and several options."
>
> Me: "Yes, I know. What kind of monthly tickets do you have?"
>
> Customer service representative: "That depends on where you want to go."

Several more rounds of this sort of exchange followed; I do genuinely believe that such an exchange could only happen in Germany. My naive hope of getting a brief overview of some passes, and maybe even a recommendation to go along with it, was shattered in seconds. A few years later during a train journey that must have broken *Deutsche Bahn's* track record (pun intended) for the most incompetent service ever provided, I asked a ticket inspector a question and stupidly expected to get an answer in return. Upon boarding a train to the charming town of Zittau in the east, I proceeded to look for my reserved seat, number 105. My first surprise was to find that seat number 105 didn't exist. The fun and games didn't end there. On this eight-hour train journey the on-board restaurant wasn't working, so no hot food or drinks were available. We were told this would be fixed by the time we reached Hamburg, so in other words, four and a half hours later, but it wasn't. As is typical on a German long-distance train, due to a technical fault, the seat reservations could not be shown. Now normally when this happens you just get to kick the person out of what should be your seat, no questions asked. But on this train, we had an additional treat in store. The train was booked out, so if you hadn't spent 5 euros to reserve yourself a seat in advance, you were told that you had to leave the train. I couldn't even console myself with the internet to pass the time, because, you guessed it, there was, as ever, no functioning internet connection (but good old *Deutsche Bahn* plans to have WLAN in all trains by 2026, so with any luck we'll have it by 2040).

No doubt had you travelled forward in time from the 1850s or from the Third World you may have considered the service a bit shabby but overall acceptable. What with all this chaos we inevitably left the starting point with quite a considerable delay. Since I had to change trains part way through the journey, I asked the inspector if I would still make my connection, and if not, what my best options were. His extremely accommodating answer came as he had already started moving away from me and down the aisle, his back turned to me and his voice not much more than a moody mumble: "You can work that out for yourself."

Ich verstehe nur Bahnhof

Since I couldn't buy any food and had no idea when I'd arrive at my destination, I started to get quite hungry and impatient. I walked up to the on-board restaurant anyway, hoping that by some small miracle there would be some food, but instead of finding a restaurant I found a man eating his own Frankfurter sausages out of a jar and staring out of the window. He saw me, put two and two together and asked if I'd like to share his sausages. Though the prospect of eating a stranger's sausages was a little awkward, not knowing when I'd next be able to eat, I accepted his kind offer. Being British I imagined that we would get talking and that this would help me get over the initial discomfort of eating someone else's sausages. After a few brief attempts at conversation the stranger made it clear that he hadn't signed up for this. He offered me sausages so we were there to eat sausages, nothing more. After what seemed an eternity of eating a stranger's food in silence, I said thank you and continued chomping in silence. As I've come to learn in Germany, every silver lining has a cloud.

After only a few minutes of this awkward silence, I decided to bite the bullet and try and break it. "I can't believe there's no functioning restaurant on board this nine-hour train journey. Have you experienced this before?"

"Jein," he answers, which is the German for "yes and no". He doesn't elaborate, so I go on.

"Do you have much further to go?"

"Weiß nett. Kommt darauf an." "I don't know, it depends."

I wasn't entirely sure what he meant here, so I took it to mean he doesn't know how much longer we'll be delayed for. I start to rack my brains for a different line of approach, but it takes me a while to figure out what to say, so I pretend to be absorbed in the landscape. The only thing I can make out though is the sausage stranger's reflection in the window, hands deep in his Frankfurter jar. I just pray that our eyes don't meet in the reflection.

There's no need to worry for much longer as the conductor comes to my rescue and announces that we'll shortly be arriving at Castrop-Rauxel, which I had up until then always believed was a name for a drug to treat the thyroid. We pull in jerkily to the station and passengers flood in, elbowing those out the way who had been standing by the doors, fingers stretched out ready to press the door opening button, for the last ten minutes. This causes yet another short delay which really riles my sausage stranger. He suddenly turns his head away from the window and looks directly at me, and imbued with a sense of courage and conviction tells me in detail about his two connections which he's now definitely going to miss, how this is frankly *"unter aller Sau"*, which means "bloody awful", but literally "under all sow" (pigs really do feature heavily in our exchange). I nod my head, not able to get a word in edgeways. He then picks up his almost empty jar of sausages and storms off.

His reaction brings me back to reality and gets me thinking about my own journey, so I make my way back to my seat and see if I can get any information from a member of staff. Walking through the busy aisles I spot a man in uniform and ask him about the likelihood of making my connection, to which he shouts, *"Hömma, ich habe keine Glaskugel"* ("Listen, I don't have a crystal ball"). Unsurprisingly, a passenger overhears this and firmly but kindly says to me *"Ruhrpott Schnauze,"* then gets back to his newspaper.

It appears there is some kind of hierarchy among Germans about where people are the rudest. In the West where I live, people complain about the *"Berliner Schnauze"*, often citing Berliners as abrupt, rude and offensive. *"Berliner Schnauze"* is basically a metaphor for "Berlin sass", but really means "Berlin rudeness". Likewise, *"Ruhrpott Schnauze"* is a metaphor for "Ruhr Valley sass", so in other words, "Ruhr Valley rudeness". Kind of rolls of the tongue, doesn't it? It is intended to be humorous; it's an insult masqueraded as humour. Perhaps Germans should make this into some kind of competition involving numerous archaically complex rules. *"Would you like to discover where in Germany are the most obnoxious and churlish inhabitants? To take part, fill in this form of 236 pages making sure to put a cross in the boxes and not a tick. Then fill it out another two times and scan it to us using your scanner from 1988. Scanners from 1989 and after will not be accepted. The first prize will be a slap in the face and the runner-up will get a year's free subscription to the Deutsche Bahn."* Or something equally painful. Feeling too demoralised to make any further attempts to find out at what time or month I'd make it to my destination, I sit back down and ponder the significance of the German phrase *"ich verstehe nur Bahnhof"*, or "it's all Greek to me" (literally, "I understand only train station").

In short, in Germany, it is generally safe to assume that the people you speak with here, particularly when wearing some kind of uniform or in some position of authority, are:

- hostile, and wish to inconvenience you to the maximum of their ability;
- about as responsive as a statue covered in moss;
- convinced that mistakes can be made to disappear by arrogantly refusing to admit they have made one;
- convinced that if you fail to notice their mistake then it's your mistake and you must pay for it.

CHAPTER 13

§450 Ich bin auch nur ein Mensch
I'm only human

❦

In my eleven years of living in Germany, I'm convinced that Elton John must have secretly dedicated his song "Sorry Seems to Be the Hardest Word" to the Germans. You'd have more chance of getting ice water from hell than an admission of wrongdoing from a German. I once had to make an appointment with the ear, nose and throat doctor to get my ears syringed.[21] On the phone the receptionist asked me for my date of birth, which I duly gave her. As you now know, most encounters with German civil servants/doctors' receptionists are about as friendly as an obese ant with lumbago carrying enormous shopping bags, and this exchange proved no different. "We can't find you on the system," she replied. This was most bizarre as I had been a patient there for years. After some exaggerated sighing at my wasting two precious minutes of her life, I was asked to repeat my date of birth.

"The 23rd of the 12th," I loudly and slowly repeated. Then, as if by magic, I suddenly showed up on the system.

"Ah," she said, "*you* said the 22nd."

I needed a few seconds to process this. If I had understood correctly, I had just been told a) what I had said, and b) I had got my birthday wrong. Now that really takes some nerve, but it wasn't an isolated experience. This must-never-admit-guilt/always-be-right

---

[21] In Germany your local GP doesn't do much bar refer you to specialists. You cannot even get your ears cleaned by a GP. Having said that, it seems that from spring 2023 GPs in the UK no longer provide the expertise or funding to carry out earwax removal services either.

attitude applies to a majority of the people in this country. In Germany when tipping at cafés and restaurants it's customary to tell the waiting staff the sum that you wish to give them, rather than leave the change on the table (presumably because this allows them to scowl at you and ruin the rest of your day if you don't give them what they feel they are entitled to get). So, when my bill once came to 17 euros 20, I said 19. My change came back at 2 euros. "I've been given too much change," I said.

"*You* said 18 euros."

This time I was happy to just pocket the extra euro and continue on my way.

In many respects, it's little wonder that Germans don't stand up to these petty, incompetent and arrogant people and corporations. I mean, the system is clearly unfairly stacked against us little people. Take my short stint of unemployment as an example. In Germany, if you have been employed for two years (twenty-four months), you are entitled to 60 per cent of your last salary for one year (only persons over fifty-eight can get benefits for two years as we know that in Germany, once you're over fifty you're half dead and hence can't get a new job). So, after working for six years on temporary contracts at various universities with no hope of anyone bending the rules on my behalf, I too found myself without work. My first instalment of money was due at the start of April 2018. When I checked my balance, nothing had come through, so I had no other recourse but to chase up the money myself. Trying to get hold of someone on the phone took an eternity, and when I finally did manage to speak to someone, the situation took a (by now) predictable twist. It turns out I had been given two different usernames. To remedy this, and to get at my money, I had to be sent – by post – a new pin code and start all over again. By this point I couldn't hide my frustration any more and wanted to know how it was possible that such a mistake could happen and go unnoticed for so long. The man on the phone had the typical get-out-of-making-an-apology answer already prepared "*ich bin auch nur ein Mensch*" ("I'm only human"). Bear in mind this excuse only applies to large corporations, however, never to individuals, and you'll hear it as a substitute for an apology whenever a representative of a faceless organisation messes up. If you're really unlucky you might hear them say, "*Das Leben ist kein*

Wunschkonzert" ("Life is no picnic"). The customer is anything but "king" in Germany.

This brings me on to another golden rule. In Germany, customer service is not customer-oriented and public services are not public-oriented. I'm only now starting to learn that to a German admitting that they're wrong is like admitting that they are no longer in control of the outcome, and the "plan" has gone to pieces (though frequently there is no real long-term plan; the three-month-long 9-euro train ticket experiment from June to August 2022 with no follow-up model is a case in point). Oftentimes I see this at work where my German colleagues completely lose it whenever their computer breaks down, someone disagrees with them, they can't figure something out or something simply doesn't go according to plan. A true German, you see, believes their day should run 100 per cent on their terms. Any infringement on their set idea of how it should run is met with a "how-dare-you" attitude. It seems that Germans just don't have that mechanism inside them that allows them to flourish in a contingency plan, to stay calm and collected under pressure, to improvise and to work out a solution with whatever tools are available. Perhaps it's due to an absolute faith in and need for authority, but openly admitting they're wrong when they've been given everything to do things right shows flaws in themselves and in the much revered "system". So, when things don't pan out as planned, expect to see a lot of headless chickens in panic mode. Much flapping of wings, prolonged hissy fits and feathers flying all over the place.

CHAPTER 14

§546 Das musst du doch wissen!
You must know that!

৵৵৵

As one of my students perceptively pointed out in a heated discussion about cycling provisions in our city, many Germans lack both the courage and the planning power to do things properly, to see a project through until the end, fearing the consequences if things go wrong and not wanting to assume responsibility. Half measures are therefore frequently taken instead. A case in point is the rolling out of an electronic patient file from January 2021. Since January 2021, German patients have the right to an electronic file. But being in Germany, it has been left up to the patients themselves to decide whether they want to take part in this or not and what information they would and wouldn't like to have in it. What's more, when doctors actually ask their patients about this potentially life-saving tool, many say they have never heard of it. Jochen Werner, the boss of Essen's university clinic and author of *So krank ist das Krankenhaus* (*So sick are our Hospitals*), states that it's typically German to think that people would just happen to know about the existence of such a thing.[22] He goes on to add that it's the same story with tax declarations, which everyone is required to fill out and even Germans themselves grapple with. In typically German fashion, people are just expected to know things and muddle through

---

[22] *So krank ist das Krankenhaus: Ein Weg zu mehr Menschlichkeit, Qualität und Nachhaltigkeit in der Medizin*, Prof. Dr Jochen A. Werner, Klartext Verlag, 2022.

somehow.[23] This really resonated with me. The patchy nature of everything here makes it so hard to find support, even if there is actually any available.

---

[23] A report recently appeared on this subject in the German magazine *Der Spiegel*. In the article entitled *Bloß nicht Deutschland! (Not Germany!)*, a major reason why qualified foreigners leave Germany is the lack of help and support on offer. The main reason for leaving as cited in the article was the fact that degrees and qualifications from abroad often aren't recognised.

CHAPTER 15

§228 Servicewüste Deutschland
Service desert Germany

ⱌᷢᷤᷠᷤᷤᷟ

If you really want to experience the oxymoron that is customer service in Germany, I strongly recommend you start with shopping. Dating back to 1956, Germany's strict store-closing law serves to show how the country's unions and shopkeepers have conspired to maintain hours that favour shop owners and workers over the customer.[24] Some small changes have been made since then, notably in 1989 with the addition of Thursday late shopping and in 1993, when shops in airports and train stations were given permission to open. Sundays still very much feel like a ghost town, but at least bakeries are open until around midday, maybe a bit later if you're lucky. The queues for the best bread start from 6 a.m. onwards. It's also not uncommon for many smaller, independent shops, post offices, chemists and banks to close between noon and 2 p.m. for a "siesta". And many bank branches are closed all day Saturday. So there goes that essential shopping in your lunch break or weekend. Admittedly, this also happens in countries like Spain, but at least in Spain they go back to work until around 8 p.m. and they actually have a climate that justifies a siesta.

In Germany shops also open quite late, between 9.30 and 10 a.m., which I found out after an early eye appointment in the town centre. I thought I'd get myself some essentials when it would still be quiet, but at 9 a.m. everything was still very much closed. But anyway, store opening hours nowadays can be one of the most baffling things you encounter here. I guess that with this relaxing of the closing law

---

[24] The so-called "Ladenschlussgesetz".

people feel they can pretty much do whatever they like, very much in keeping with the German mentality. I have a few favourite independent cafés and second-hand stores here, but I very rarely go, as I just happen to find the opening hours of Tuesdays to Thursdays 11 a.m.–1 p.m. and 3–5 p.m., Fridays 3–6 p.m. and Saturdays 12–4.15 p.m. somewhat difficult to remember and fit in around my work. I've come to the conclusion that many people treat their shops and stores as a hobby.

If you do happen to remember the opening hours of a café and manage to pop in occasionally, don't be too surprised if you get something completely different to what you ordered. The laws of customer service here stipulate that the customer is irrelevant. On a recent trip to the lovely city of Leipzig I stumbled across a cute café and fancied stopping for a cup of Earl Grey. The menu told me I could order black tea or herbal tea. When the waitress finally comes over, she slowly and begrudgingly takes my order:

Me: "I'd like a cup of Earl Grey, please."

Waitress: "Darjeeling." She notes it down as she says it.

Me: "Sorry, I said Earl Grey."

Waitress: "We don't have Earl Grey."

And that, ladies and gentlemen, is how you win over new customers.

Sarcasm off. Once you are familiar with the sheer absence of service, inconvenience of shopping and difficulty in ordering a basic refreshment, you might wish to step it up a bit and get yourself a mobile phone contract or gym membership. Then you can experience the land of self-renewing contracts and all the joys that entails. As a general rule, unless specifically told otherwise, assume that *any* contract or subscription will auto renew. It's really quite a clever and effective consumer scam when you think about it, and I've been on the receiving end several times. It does make total German sense though, as companies can rely on income from people who forget to cancel and they don't have to improve their service or products. When I had a two-and-a-half-hour commute for one of my university posts I splashed out on a German railcard 50, so a railcard giving me 50 per cent off long-distance journeys. A month before my university contract expired, I decided to write to *Deutsche Bahn* to cancel it. But, as with everything in Germany, it wasn't that straightforward. My card had automatically been renewed for one year as I hadn't cancelled it six weeks (at the latest) before the expiry date. I didn't know that I had to, but in Germany ignorance is no excuse, so I ended up paying 247 euros for a card that I barely used. German Rail: 1, consumer: 0.

As Germans are also very good at being sneaky and secretive, a word of advice from me is to carefully check the *exact* duration of any contract you receive. In particular, gyms have perfected the art of messing with their customers. It's getting increasingly common to make gym memberships twenty-two months, rather than twenty-four months, which is what the average person would naturally expect. The intention here is clear. Companies can bank on their customers assuming that it's a two-year contract thereby making it impossible for them to cancel on time. There is some good news, however, and it does seem that Germany is now finally trying to join other developed countries and offer something resembling a service. In March 2022 a new law stipulated that these self-renewing contracts were to be abolished, yet it can still take more than six months to close a bank account. This law change might be great for those who took out a contract after May and who can benefit from a contract fit for developed-world conditions. For those already locked into a contract, it's a more dismal picture.

Yet the award for the most agonising and incompetent experience when unsubscribing *and* being reimbursed goes to a renowned German telecoms operator beginning with T. Getting good customer service in Germany is about as likely as seeing the sun in an English summer. As I had to be out of my last flat by December 2020, I took up my first contact with the telecoms company around September of that year, informing them that I would be moving in three months and needed to cancel my contract. I naively hoped that three months would be enough time to get things sorted. By January 2023 the job still hadn't been completed correctly. The first kick in the teeth was the news that I couldn't get out of my contract before October 2021, as that was the official date of the end of my contract. So, begrudgingly, I continued to pay somewhere in the region of 53 euros a month for ten months for a service I was no longer receiving. In Germany this is par for the course.

Fast-forward to October 2021 when I am sent a letter confirming that my contract will be terminated that month. Fast-forward another month, and guess what? My bank statement reveals that the telecoms company have taken 53 euros out of my account. So off I go to the company website to find a name of someone I can email to ask what the heck is going on. This is when I see that the website publishes no contact details of individuals you can write to; the only option is to fill out a contact form. Finding the right contact form takes a fair amount of time and patience, and while searching there is no end to the number of pop-ups which appear on your screen asking you to call someone. Of course, it's much better to call as then the company can fob you off more easily. I manage to fill out contact form number one of about twenty so far. You see, Germans don't like writing emails and in several cases companies and especially authorities will go as far as to not publish any contact details on their websites so that they have no accountability when what they tell you turns out to be nonsense. At the start of February, I had a text message from the telecoms company telling me that "my enquiry had been dealt with". I filled out another contact form to find out what was meant by this. The answer? The completely random sum of 14 euros and 96 cents has now been reimbursed. If I'd asked my four-year-old nephew to do the maths here, I would have been surprised at the answer, but this is coming from a supposedly reputable company. Simply put, there is no meaningful tracking of contact. Call backs don't happen, conversations are not recorded and every contact essentially means starting the whole process again.

Chapter 16

§314 Sie müssen sofort zahlen!
You have to pay immediately!

ༀ᠆ᠬ

One of the golden rules to remember about life in Germany is this: *every time you leave your house, someone is after your money.* Repeat and learn. For no apparent reason in Germany, unjustifiable extra fees are levied on people on an almost daily basis. Be it your bank account, which charges you anywhere in the region of 3 and 10 euros for the privilege of having an account; be it any faceless corporation that sends you a *"Mahnung"* (written reminder) before you have received a bill[25]; be it your health insurance company that doesn't reimburse treatment, this is a fact of life in Germany and it is not challenged by your average Hermann.

At the start of 2019, my local bank, which also conveniently happens to be one of the most popular in Germany, started charging for online accounts. Just like that, because it felt like it. It now costs around 3.63 euros, whereas it was originally free. Another sting is having to pay around 1 euro to withdraw your own money. Luckily mine is one of the branches which doesn't charge customers for this, but it really is a lottery out there. Out of approximately 400 branches nationwide, forty or more charge you to take out your own money, some of which every time, others only every third time. What's more, the charges differ depending on which part of Germany you live in. Oftentimes only employees with a net salary in excess of 2,000, 2,500 or 3,000 euros can get a fee-free account, and if you have less than 1,200 euros a month going into your account you can expect to pay

---

[25] German companies are very quick to send you scary and incomprehensible overdue notices. The problem is, they frequently come before the actual bill.

more. The poor are punished in Germany. One thing that all banks have in common, however, is that it is seen as the customer's responsibility to print out their bank statements once a month at their local branch. If Hermann fails to do this then the bank has no choice but to print it out for him and bill him for the postage. That'll teach him! Although the bank ought to be obliged to reimburse these scandalous and unjustifiable fees, it may only do so if the consumer explicitly demands it. And how many little German lambs do you think a) will actually know about this, and b) will go ahead and challenge it? At the start of 2021 when my local gem of a bank wrote to its customers asking for a hefty 9 euros a month for a bank account instead of the 7 euros we had been paying, over 90 per cent of people didn't challenge it.[26]

Hand in hand with being ripped off by your local bank is an utter disregard for customer loyalty. Loyalty doesn't pay, even if you have a very healthy bank account. On numerous occasions there have been reports of customers who have received a letter from their bank telling them they were closing their account. No explanation was provided. And they were the lucky ones. One lady found herself unable to pay for her groceries in a supermarket as her account had been closed and they didn't bother to inform her. No doubt she wasn't the only one. What is truly sickening about this is that, by law, private banks don't have to give a reason for randomly closing accounts here. According to a newspaper article on this very topic, the main reason why these private banks do this is that they don't make enough profit out of the customer in question.[27] One poor sod paid an eye-watering 34.90 euro a month for a premium business account only for his account to be closed three months later.[28]

Something else which many Germans also unquestioningly take up the backside is the laughably poor interest rates. As it now stands, the most interest you can get on a current account is 1 per cent. Hardcore. For the majority of accounts, though, you get 0.001 per

---

[26] https://www.handelsblatt.com/finanzen/banken-versicherungen/banken/kontofuehrungsgebuehren-sparkassen-holen-sich-ueber-90-prozent-zustimmung-/28834602.html
[27] https://www.nordbayern.de/wirtschaft/plotzlich-ohne-konto-commerzbank-kundigt-nurnbergerinnen-ohne-grund-1.10997023
[28] https://www.modern-banking.de/ebg_cob.php

cent or 0.00 per cent, so I guess those making a whopping 1 per cent should just shut up and enjoy the privilege. When it comes to savings accounts, currently 1 per cent is the highest on offer, again with most banks paying out 0.01 per cent interest.[29] If you need to get hold of a bank statement dating back several months, let's say because you need to check that company X didn't rip you off five months ago, you're pretty much screwed. Most bank accounts only give you a three-month history, and, in perfect keeping with the money-grabbing mentality, it costs to get anything older. With online banking it's somewhat more in line with the twenty-first century and you can get statements for up to one year. It's still very limited when I compare it with NatWest in the UK, which allowed me to go back seven years. Charging for older reprints is of course a tidy little business, but for the customer, a very poor show.

Only in Germany

As if it's not bad enough getting no interest whatsoever, good old oh-so-customer-friendly German banks recently introduced *negative* interest. Yippee! Banks were charging 0.5 per cent for sums beyond 50,000 euros (25,000 for some banks). Thankfully this scandalous practiced stopped around the end of 2022. I've now reached the stage where I really wonder what "services" are actually being provided to offset all of this. Take bank opening times. My bank opening hours make Berlin airport, the airport that took fourteen years to construct, look like a paragon of success. In my part of town, the bank is open from 9.30 a.m., closes again at 12.30 p.m., has a one-and-a-half-hour lunch break, then reopens at 2 p.m. till 4 p.m. On Thursdays you can benefit from longer opening hours where the bank closes at 6 p.m. On Saturdays – the day when most people have time to go to the bank – it's closed all day, including the main branch in the city centre.

The most recent stunt which my bank has pulled is, I strongly believe, one which could not happen in any other country. A few months ago, a letter arrived from my bank, written in the usual

---

[29] https://www.weltsparen.de/geldanlage/sparkonto/#:~:text=Die%20Zinsen%20f%C3%BCr%20klassische%20Sparkonten,deutlich%20h%C3%B6here%20Zinsen%20zu%20erzielen.

long-winded and deliberately complicated style. In a nutshell, the bank wants to inform their customers that they will be making changes to their terms and conditions. They would like us to let them know whether we will agree to these changes. Now, here's the rub; anywhere else in the civilised world, you would get to see which terms they were changing and then what they will be replacing them with. Not here. In Hermann's world, we are not explicitly told what the terms and conditions are; rather we are told to go and look them up ourselves, read and understand them and then tell the bank what we would like (them) to do.

Remember what Jochen Werner, author of *So krank ist das Krankenhaus* said? In Germany people are left to figure things out and muddle through alone. It gets even worse when you factor in that this is coming from a bank that prides itself on its transparency. *Repeat and learn – when in Germany you have to do everybody else's job too.*

CHAPTER 17

§719 Ich bin immer pünktlich!
I'm always on time!

❧

No one stands up to the *Deutsche Bahn* either, because it's not worth it. Consider these facts: if a train is between sixty and 119! minutes late, you can claim up to 25 per cent of the ticket price. If it's more than two hours late you can claim up to 50 per cent. As most people rightly feel that it's not worth the hassle and paperwork for such a small return, they don't contest it, and thus the *Deutsche Bahn* gets away with its appalling service.

I once had a three-month semester break from my university teaching and I thought this might give me enough time to apply for a refund after yet another horrific experience playing musical trains. Coming home from work one evening I arrived at the station to see that my train was delayed by thirty minutes. Nothing new there. Thirty minutes later there was an announcement that my train was leaving from a different platform. Off I marched with countless others to another platform, waited there for ten minutes only to be told that the train was now leaving from the platform it was originally scheduled to leave from. I filed for compensation and was sent a coupon to the value of 10 euros – it wasn't exactly the compensation I was hoping for, but it was better than waiting another six months only to be told I'm entitled to nothing. Now, here's the thing, the *Deutsche Bahn* website only accepts coupons with seven characters, and the one the *Deutsche Bahn* sent me had eight characters, so the paper wasn't even worth the money it was printed on. So, here's a little tip if ever you want to try your luck with a train journey in Germany: buy a day pass or day return from a vendor at the station rather than at a ticket machine. At vending machines, the ticket will be stamped as valid, therefore not refundable if the train gets cancelled or disappears down a black hole. If a vendor sells it to you, it won't be validated until you stamp it yourself. You can therefore hold on to it and use it for another journey, or so a good friend tells me. It might also be wise to avoid the town of Mannheim, where more than one in two trains are late.

I thought things were taking a turn for the better when *Deutsche Bahn* announced a ground-breaking plan to synchronise long-distance and regional transport so trains would run every half hour in both rural and urban areas. But it looks like the *Bahn* bit off more than it could chew. This plan has just been put back from 2030 to 2070. In 2012, 20.9 per cent of long-distance trains were late. This went up to over 24 per cent in 2018, meaning that only around 76 per cent of trains were punctual. And this punctuality rate has been getting steadily worse ever since, culminating in a pathetic 65.2 per cent of long-distance trains being punctual in 2022.

Chariots of doom are therefore not worth the hassle and are to be avoided at all costs. It's hardly surprising that, despite offering reduced train tickets since 2022, car consumption is actually on the increase. Currently there are 580 cars per 1,000 inhabitants, up from 517 cars in 2011, despite the fact that everyone's always banging on about how environmentally friendly they are. Flying unfortunately fares no better, however. I could tell you here about all my mishaps and adventures at German airports but as that would be another book, I'll leave it up to the statistics. In the local newspaper, *General Anzeiger,* which every dutiful citizen is expected to read in order to be kept up to date, a study was carried out measuring the numbers of flights from major European airports which were delayed by at least fifteen minutes, starting with June 2017 and then comparing this to delays one year later in June 2018. On this list which contains eleven airports (Amsterdam, Barcelona, Berlin, Düsseldorf, Frankfurt, London, Madrid, Moscow, Munich, Paris and Rome), Frankfurt is the clear winner with 50.2 per cent of flights leaving late in 2018, up from 33.8 per cent in 2017. This beats Paris with 43.5 per cent and London with 24.8 per cent of delayed flights in 2018. I feel it says a lot that out of eleven cities four of them are located in Germany.

Even though travelling on public transport is only for masochists, the German government is trying to force people to abandon their cars and take these chariots of doom which were subject to over 80,000 disruptions in 2022. Gentle encouragement, or soliciting the public's views first, perhaps coupled with an incentive, is not the German way. Things must instead be done with force and there must be a hefty punishment, as that's how you'll get Hermann to toe the line. Up until 2023, for example, residents of Düsseldorf could get an annual parking spot for 30 euros. Since the start of 2023 it costs 360 euros. In Berlin, an annual spot used to cost 10.20 euros. Now it's 120 euros. In the city of Bonn, 700 parking spaces have been scrapped and parking in the city centre is astronomical. People are being forced out of their cars, which may not be altogether a bad thing from an environmental perspective, but when there are no functioning alternatives, people won't be in any hurry to stop using them.

Alle Straßen führen nach Boppard

I won't even mention German drivers, bar a quote from a good friend of mine who pointed out that "Germans do not park their cars; they strategically abandon them." He then went on to add that the word "strategically" can often be dropped. Life is also tough for motorists here though; I should perhaps cut them some slack. If it's not all the hidden radars causing them no end of grief, it'll no doubt be the lack of information and signs.[30] I'll never forget the time my dad and brother came to visit me for a long weekend on the Rhine. My father decided to hire a car so we could explore and get around. One day we went to the charming city of Koblenz, saw a few gorgeous castles perched up on the vineyards, had a great meal washed down with a delicious glass of Riesling and a velvety coffee to finish, then made our way back home. Or at least tried to. You see, what we didn't know at the time was that, upon exiting the city, all roads seemed to lead to the tourist town of Boppard. Finding out where we needed to be proved a damn sight harder. After a while driving round in circles Dad decided to hand me a map and ask me

---

[30] George Mikes tells a wonderful anecdote about trying to find Bonn airport. See *Über Alles: Germany Explored*, George Mikes, Penguin Books, 1969. Go to the chapter entitled "Bonn".

to direct him. I did my best and two minutes later we ended up back where we started: staring at yet another Boppard sign.

Convinced I couldn't read maps properly and quickly running out of patience, Dad pulled over and examined it himself instead. Off we go again only to end up where I had just directed him; either we were going crazy or all roads really did lead to Boppard. It was about as difficult to find the right exit as it was trying to leave the UK in January 2021 during lockdown. Five minutes and ten Boppard signs later we finally came across the sign we were looking for and got home with a delay of only two hours.

CHAPTER 18

§529 Digitalisierung in Deutschland
"Digitalisation" in Germany

ᔕᙅᔓ

Another golden rule to remember about life in Germany is that German law often favours a company over the consumer. Though I had been warned about lack of service and professionalism by a major leading internet provider in Germany (you know the one. It begins with a "T"), I was still flabbergasted when a colleague told me about his ordeal trying to get the internet installed at his place. He bought a package deal on 2 February 2013 and was told the installation appointment would be for 3 March, between 12 and 6 p.m., so a mere month later. On the 2 March he received a letter saying the appointment had been postponed until 10 March (no reason provided). Come the 10 March my friend stays at home all day only for nobody to turn up. He called up the company and was told that the service person didn't have time that day (again, no reason given). Fast-forward to 13 March when he comes home to a note that they tried to call at 4 p.m. but nobody was at home. He wanted to know why a technician came with no appointment, but you guessed it, no explanation was given. There were a few more stages of this, finishing with a technician coming and, rather than ringing the bell, deciding to wait outside for the door to be opened to him, and then leaving when no one came. I never found out what the end of this story was; I was too embarrassed to ask. It's 2024 now, so, who knows, maybe he finally has internet at his place.

I once had a problem with my mobile phone. When I went to the local store to get assistance the guy in the customer service department told me, "I don't have that problem with my phone." That was a load off my mind. As with banking, when it comes to phones and the internet, Germany is stuck in a time warp. Internet here is often very slow and the reception leaves a lot to be desired – don't even bother trying to use it on a high-speed train. An article published in 2013 (though I very much doubt that anything has changed since then) stated that 90 per cent of users get around 6 megabytes per second.[31] This has left Germany behind Hungary and Poland. Why is it so slow and backward in Germany? Because the big providers invest far too little in technology and broadband infrastructure. As always, it comes down to that all important question of money.

Only in Germany

As we should know by now, German transport is far from all it's cracked up to be. It's even Germany's dirty little secret. So, you'd imagine that if you can't get to work one day on time or at all as these chariots of doom are on strike, you may as an employee have some options? Wrong. In Germany, a public transportation strike is not a valid excuse to come late to work.[32] Hermann must be on time! Employers can legally cut pay in the short run, and if the problem repeats, they can impose stronger sanctions. If you know in advance that there is going to be a strike you can a) find someone to drive you to work, b) take a taxi to work at your own cost, or c) stay in a hotel near your place of work. So much for the highly lauded German workers' rights. One day I decided to integrate the topic of transport strikes into a few of my lessons, just to sound people out and to see what their take on all of this was. Not a single person had any objections to the above. One lady said that it's the employee's responsibility to get to work; her argument being that the employee knows how long it will take and how difficult it will be to get to work when they sign their contract, so they should plan for this. In another class several students had taken unpaid vacation days when they couldn't make it in to work due to a strike.

---

[31] *Die Schmalband-Republik*, Konrad Lischka and Ole Reißmann, *Der Spiegel*, 21.06.2013.
[32] https://www.spiegel.de/karriere/zu-spaet-im-buero-das-muessen-pendler-wissen-a-1070316.html, 04.01.2016.

CHAPTER 19

§384 *Vertrauen ist gut, Anwalt ist besser*[33]
Trust is good, a lawyer is better

༄༅

Whereas everyone is out to get your money here, it's extremely difficult to obtain money that is rightfully yours. Especially when you live in a country where information is hard to come by or non-existent to those without fat wallets. A case in point is having to pay 200 euros for an appointment to talk about pension plans with the *"Verbraucherzentrale"*, the German citizens advice bureau. People who work in universities and schools in Germany are paid according to a fixed pay scale, which should in theory make life less complicated. Typically, as a new teacher or lecturer you start off on level one and then over time, with experience, your pay goes up to the next level and continues until your reach the maximum level.

While working at the vocational college I needed to dig out a payslip for my flat search and I just happened to see that I was down as level three. The rules stipulate that after three years on level three, you automatically move up to level four, but by this stage I had been on level three for three years and five months. I contacted the college about this to see if they could correct my pay. Surprisingly, I got a positive answer: yes, I would be put on level four starting the next month. However, I was not allowed to claim back the difference over the past five months. My astonishment was exacerbated by the fact that TV and health insurance companies can backtrack up to *six months* to get missed payments from their customers, yet I was

---

[33] Taken and modified from the original quotation, *"Vertrauen ist gut, Kontrolle ist besser"*. (Trust is good, control is better.) You'll see this slogan plastered over trams advertising the service of lawyers.

unable to claim for money that I had rightfully earned. Moreover, only from 2018 were health insurance companies legally bound to reimburse overpaid health insurance![34] Prior to that they just pocketed Hermann's cash. It turns out that there is a law which screws over employees here, and again, it is largely shrouded in mystery (well, my friend who has a German law degree didn't know about it, neither did my colleagues at the college).

Once again, little Hermann finds himself crushed by the system. Apparently, there is such a thing in employment contracts as an "*Ausschlussfrist*", which translates as "cut-off period" or, from the Latin, "term of preclusion". It mainly applies to requests for salary increases, payment of overtime, and holiday allowance and it means that after a certain amount of time has passed, typically a minimum of three months, any of the above requests are no longer valid if they have not been requested beforehand in writing. And of course, they won't have been requested beforehand as nobody tells you anything here. There are no consequences for the employer though if they happen to oversee something.

Dealing with tax returns in Germany is another area in which the individual is largely left to figure out other people's errors and fend for themselves in an incomprehensible maze of endless exceptions and possible deductions, as our dear friend Jochen Werner rightly alluded to. Below is a small sample of perhaps not-so-obvious tax-deductible expenses in Germany:

- Income related expenses – if an expense is partly related to your income and partly to your private life, you can make a claim. Provided the private element can be clearly accounted for and separated.
- Relocation – anything in relation to your move to Germany.
- Church tax (in other words, that tax that is automatically deducted from your salary and which you can only stop by formally opting out of paying).

---

[34] https://uepo.de/2017/11/05/neu-ab-2018-krankenkassenbeitraege-werden-rueckwirkend-angepasst-und-zu-viel-gezahlte-beitraege-erstattet/#:~:text=Neu%2 0ist%2C%20dass%20zu%20viel,waren%2C%20wird%20die%20Beitragsdifferenz% 20nachgefordert.

- Home office –a separate room in your home can be claimed if it is used as the centre of your work and you have no other work place. But note: this only counts if you have an extra room to use as an office.
- Clothing – not your typical smart suit, tie and shirt, but clothing which can *only* be used for work, such as in labs and on building sites.
- Books, journals, and publications related to your work.
- Professional membership fees.
- Customer entertainment – invitations to lunch or dinner with current or potential customers and anyone of use to you in relation to your current or future work are tax deductible. Seventy per cent of the bill can be claimed if you can provide the receipt with the names of people present and the reason. (I now know why my freelancing colleague always used to pay for our meals upfront then get me to pay him in cash while he asked for a receipt. He was a real rock that guy.)
- MBA course fees.
- Banking fees.
- Donations.
- Binoculars, whip, handcuffs – if you can explain how they relate to your work, you can get some money back.

A general rule is that provided you can make your claim plausible, the link between your work situation and the expense credible, it's worth trying your luck and making a claim as it's highly unlikely to be rejected. Unlike in the UK, where the employer takes care of filing tax returns at no cost for the employee, in Germany it's solely the individual's responsibility to take care of this. But beware: no one tells you that this is the case; for when in Germany you should know. I once read a statistic that 80 per cent of all published tax law is in German – now you know why the rich in Germany pay no tax; the law is so complex that a good tax advisor can run rings around the authorities.

I had been here for over a year when the secretary at the university I was working at asked me how I got on with my tax return for 2013. Somewhat shocked, I replied that I didn't have a clue what she was talking about. Seeing that I turned a nasty shade of pale, she tried to calm me down and kindly told me about a little-known organisation that helps people with their tax returns for a reasonable annual fee. The so-called *"Lohnsteuerhilfevereine"* (Income Tax Help Associations) are everywhere in Germany and work out much cheaper than getting a tax advisor. For one year you can have unlimited phone calls, emails, advice and what's more you pay in accordance with your wages. It really can be a life-saver. Yet, in many respects, my experience of being a customer with such an association left a lot to be desired. I managed to find myself an advisor; a larger-than-life figure with an interesting dialect and an even more interesting collection of empty toilet rolls in his bathroom, arranged in a neat pyramid and lovingly labelled "Jochen's artwork" by his wife.

In the tax year of 2018, when I had spent four months unemployed, I was happy to hear that, according to his estimations, I would get somewhere in the region of 1,750 euros reimbursed. Perhaps I should have had my doubts, though. Not infrequently would he get angry with the computer and shout out *"Wat soll der Käse?"* ("What is this crap?") I started to count how many times he would say this during a consultation to make the time pass more quickly. Fast-forward two weeks to a letter from the finance office telling me that I am to be reimbursed to the tune of 119 euros. Checking through their sums I saw that I had been listed as having an office in my home, which is, and never has been, the case. Once that mistake was sorted, I lost a further 20 euros. Still not happy with this huge discrepancy I wrote to my tax advisor to see whether he could account for it.

"Could you send me your documents again? I wasn't able to read everything," was his response. The remaining 1,650 euros never appeared in my account.

CHAPTER 20

§190 Ich war es nicht
It wasn't me

❦

After spending eleven years in Germany, I'm now petrified of having any kind of misfortune and have, as a consequence, stopped leaving my flat. Indeed, I almost have a mini-breakdown every time I see a letter accompanied with this symbol: §. It isn't the thought of catching Covid that's doing it. It's rather the fear of languishing in a police cell, or paying a fine amounting to more than an average life insurance payout. You see, if I don't have a thousand different types of insurance, I'm easy prey for the typical German waiting to sue me for the most minor thing. Everybody who comes to Germany should obviously know that according to SGB §48 Para 24a, subsection e *"you will need third-party liability insurance to provide cover to you or any other insured member of your family in the event that you commit an act for which a German court would consider you normally negligent"*.[35] It's blatantly obvious, right? This includes injuries or damage caused to animals. Under German law, there is no ceiling on the level of damages an individual could have awarded against them, including one committed innocently but carelessly.

The worrying thing about all of this, in particular when you consider the example of third-party or personal liability insurance, is that accidents are treated as fault and there is a punitive impact on society. It's the principle rather than the cost that's the problem here. Paying somewhere in the region of 7 euros a month for your

---

[35] Quotation taken from howtogermany.com (Insurance in Germany), referencing details invented for fun.

personal liability insurance is not the end of the world. The real problem is instead a system set out to create monetary settlements instead of instilling logic in people, which to my mind only serves to establish a culture of distrust and suspicion.

This brings me on to one of my favourite pastimes – watching Germans and their finger-pointing. The two go together like Tweedledum and Tweedledee. It was a former German Foreign Minister, Klaus Kinkel who was quoted in the *Welt am Sonntag* as saying "when a German falls over, he doesn't get up right away but looks around to see who owes him compensation". In Germany, accidents don't just happen. Someone is *always* responsible. I was once trying but failing to mingle at a conference when I overheard two women talking about an acquaintance who wanted to be reimbursed around 300 euros. It turned out that she had invited friends around for an evening, and one lady spilt some white wine on her couch. I was tempted to intervene and ask why this person served people wine on a couch she prises so dearly, but I bit my tongue. Normally such "issues" could be settled with a bit of flexible thinking, or heaven forbid, common sense. I mean, surely if you invite people into your house and serve alcohol you understand there is a risk that accidents might happen, right? Wrong. Instead, you should fall back on the logic that in Germany everybody must watch what they're doing and people should know better than to have simple accidents.

I'm still grappling with the idea here of not taking responsibility for yourself and realising that sometimes accidents just happen. The need to go to court for something, to go after people for little things, and not to work stuff out amongst yourselves is hard to comprehend. It's *always* someone's fault, especially when money is up for grabs. I'll never forget that time I was waiting for an Erasmus student of mine to come and see me in my office hour. She was late, which wasn't like her. When she finally turned up, she was a bit of a sight for sore eyes, and that's putting it mildly. She got pushed trying to get into the tram on her way to my office, she then fell over and was trampled on. She left this tram and entered a second one, limping and in obvious pain. Not a single person asked her how she was or if she needed help. Shortly after I watched a programme on exactly this theme; the show had actors fall down in front of people in cafés, bars, etc. and watch how people responded. When questioned why they didn't intervene to help, the most common answers were a) the accident didn't affect me, b) the accident was their own fault as they weren't wearing the right shoes, and c) I'm scared I'll worsen the condition by helping as I'm not medically trained. So, when some time later I saw a woman fall off her moped in Bonn I was curious to see which of the above scenarios she'd be a victim of. A good twenty or so people stood around to watch while one kind soul helped her up. Once she was back on her feet and able to push the moped around the corner, at least three of the people who were gawping at her during the accident took the time to tell her that she wasn't allowed to have the moped on the pavement.

CHAPTER 21

§279 Es ist billig, in Deutschland zu leben!

It's cheap living in Germany!

⌒⌒⌒

The average Hermann is too far buried in his shell of resignation and acceptance of being mistreated to really get his Lederhosen in a twist about the various daily injustices and demands for your money here. In pretty much no other area of life is this injustice more clearly seen than when dealing with the German *"Makler"*, or estate agent. If you collect enough tokens on a cereal packet, you too can send off to become a *Makler*. Whereas you pretty much need a piece of paper to show you can wipe your arse in Germany, there is bizarrely no certification necessary to become a *Makler*. A cursory glance at a well-known estate agent website confirms this. Just get your head around this: to become a *Makler* you need neither training, nor a university degree, nor a school leaving certificate (!).[36] Indeed, as the site says, "anyone can become a Makler", and that has been my experience so far.

It is somewhat paradoxical that in a nation where people tend to be extremely reluctant to part with their cash, Germans are happy to fork out on both insurance schemes and *Maklers*. This is how it works with renting here: once a *Makler* has found a tenant, he then takes his whopping 2.38 months' rent and disappears. There is no property management involved, no recommendations

---

[36] https://www.mcmakler.de/verkaufen/immobilienmakler-werden

of properties which match your requests and no being taken around properties to view beforehand. A *Makler* simply puts up an advert online and tells all interested to come for a viewing, say on Saturday at 12 p.m. He then stands around, answers no questions, repeats what you read on the advert and just hands out forms where you can declare your finances. Roughly the top five earners based on these forms will be passed on to the landlord who makes a final decision. And there you have it. That's how the *Makler* earns approximately 2,200 euros.

Renting a property in Germany comes with even more hidden costs than this though, would you believe? It's still the case today that many flats don't come with a kitchen or even a sink; flats in the state of North Rhine-Westphalia certainly don't, yet I've heard that in Berlin and other cities you can get an equipped kitchen. Flats are generally rented out bare, certainly without furniture and most definitely without curtains, light fixtures, and (mostly) a kitchen. Furnished flats are a lot more expensive to rent. Typically, you can expect to have a toilet, a bathroom sink, a shower, hot water, and the rest is up to you. The couple who rented the flat before me (the new one) even took the light bulbs with them. Once you factor in the cost of a *Makler*[37], a kitchen, a (typically) two-month deposit and a month's rent in advance, you're looking at around 6,000 euros before you've even moved in. And yet most Germans are still reluctant to buy. Here's a little breakdown of costs:

Makler fees: 2,200
Kitchen: 1,500
Two months' rent deposit: 1,500
One month's rent in advance: 750
Total: 5,950 euros

---

[37] I should probably point out here that you don't have to use the "services" of a *Makler* to rent a flat in Germany. You can do it alone. Which basically amounts to the same thing.

And this, or something very similar, is what you're going to get for your almost 6,000 euros:

This begs an important question: are most Germans really so cheap that they feel they have to strip the place bare and leave it looking as though crackheads were searching for copper wire to sell? The thing is though, the system here encourages penny-pinching when renting. Just consider the fact that it's the tenant's responsibility to paint the flat when moving out so it's all shiny and nice for the landlord. The tenant ultimately finances the flat and carries out the necessary maintenance. If you arrive in a bare flat after having firstly spent a shedload of money on redecorating the flat you've just moved out of, then forking out a ton for the deposit, and finally spending a mini-fortune on essential furniture so that you can enjoy luxuries, such as being able to cook and see in the dark, is it any wonder that people think of saving every single penny and doing something as stingy as taking the light bulbs with them? I'm surprised landlords don't ask you to reapply tar to the roof and pave the driveway after pulling up all the weeds before moving out. And getting deposits back here is also a massive struggle and is in no way guaranteed.

Landlords can withhold a deposit for six months. There is no law stipulating how long landlords can keep the deposit, because why would you have laws when you actually need them? In my case, I never got the deposit back. Not a single penny. In keeping with the tight-fisted and money-grabbing attitude Mrs Bouquet exemplified all along (did I mention that her husband has his own doctor's surgery in Switzerland but lives in Germany?), she made a fuss about giving me my money back. In the end (as I knew I'd never see my deposit again), I told her to sort out the painting and decorating herself and take it out of my deposit. She had no quibbles with that suggestion whatsoever.

So far, I would say that my flat search in Germany has been a microcosm of life here. Fake flats and scammers feature highest on the list, shortly followed by landlords and agencies who don't communicate, won't keep to the arrangement and don't tell you why, followed by an aversion to anything or anyone who's different. My first response to an advert was nothing other than massively offensive. To my email enquiry I got the following response: "*Do you have German citizenship? Do you have a permanent job? A steady income? No debts? Then get in touch.*" Once I'd recovered from the shock of this blatant discrimination my email provider notified me of two flat scams involving Airbnb. I had enquired about two furnished flats in my town, to which I got lengthy and helpful responses (at this stage I should have twigged that something was amiss). In both emails I was asked to pay the deposit first to an Airbnb agent as the landlord/tenant lived abroad and couldn't show me the flat. Then, if I didn't like the flat the money would be refunded to my account. Of course, I knew this couldn't be for real. But then more subtle scams followed. For three flat enquiries, again all of which were fully furnished (I'm thinking that's the moral of the story here – there are no flats with actual furniture up for grabs) I again received warning emails, telling me that this message was untrustworthy and/or the person behind the messages had broken the rules of the website. So, with my hopes once again dashed, I reluctantly continued to look for properties, which was when I stumbled upon, horror of horrors, the German *Makler*.

Before you hear a bit about the horrors of the *Makler*, here's a word of warning to avoid being royally scammed. Most fake ads have a preference for the number "650" and typically this is what they will state as the rent. Second, most scammers say that the flat comes fully furnished, which as I have come to learn, is about as likely as finding a non-renewing gym contract. Third and finally, the scammer provides no details of the property whatsoever. Don't say you haven't been warned.

The first *Makler* I encountered was incapable of providing the most basic of services right from the get-go. Before meeting us for a viewing he wanted to save himself some time, effort and work and sort us into groups of rich and poor at the outset. He sent around a form in which we were to declare our income and provide some other (purely) financial information. It was a PDF so I couldn't edit it. When I asked if I could receive a word document I was told "it's not possible". But at least this *Makler* was able to read emails. Regarding the second *Makler*, I decided that I no longer wanted to view the flat on offer, so I wrote to her to cancel the viewing. Two days later I got an email from her saying that, unfortunately, my scheduled viewing would no longer take place. Either she hadn't even read the email I sent, or simply didn't care as she'd clearly found someone else but didn't want to be honest and say so. The third *Makler* was without a doubt the dodgiest. Waiting outside a flat with three other viewers one day a man pulled up in the latest model Porsche. Out he stepped wearing bright yellow trousers coupled with fake snakeskin shoes. Without further ado he pushed a contract into our hands and told us to have a quick read through while looking at the property. Something in this contract startled me, so once back home I checked and found out the clause was illegal. Then, to my even greater surprise, I learnt that it's not uncommon for Germans to have entirely illegal clauses in their contracts, which is why there is always a clause saying that if any part of the contract is found to be illegal this does not invalidate the whole contract. After then leaving us to our own devices, playing with his phone and being generally unavailable and evasive, I wouldn't have been surprised to see him quietly slither out the back door.

Other common tactics here are mass viewings, and I have heard of several people getting a flat only because they were able to pay multiple months' rent upfront. This not being an option for me, I asked around how friends and colleagues managed to find a flat. A piece of advice I often heard was to provide personal and professional information about myself, a kind of biography.[38] I didn't want to have to behave as if I were applying for a job interview, but I was pretty desperate so I gave it a try. Shortly after I bagged myself a viewing, and thankfully not a mass one, of a flat a couple of bus stops away from me. The flat was quite small and dark, and being aware of this, the landlady invited me to stay and chat on the spacious and green terrace where I could fall for the charms of the place. Out on the terrace the landlady opened up a bit and ended up broaching the topic of the dreaded Brexit. She confessed that she was very hesitant to arrange a viewing for me because she didn't know whether I would be legally allowed to continue working in Germany. I told her that I was coming up to nine years here, that I was eligible for a residency permit, and my work status would not be affected. This didn't do much to put her at ease, however. In the end she asked me to get a signed letter from my employer stating that my position was permanent and that Brexit would not harm my residency. After a few raised eyebrows and head scratching from my boss, I managed to get her a signed letter. And it was only pure chance, given my job (mis)adventures, that at this particular time I had a job contract for a permanent position at the vocational college with Ms Ticking-time-bomb and co. Despite my jumping through hoops, the landlady turned me down nonetheless. As setbacks were nothing new to me by now, I found the energy to keep on writing applications and biographies for other flats of interest.

The prize for the strangest experience has to go to a sixty-something-year-old landlord who wasn't really out to rent a flat. I've heard that Germans are both perfectionists and honest. Unfortunately, those who are perfectionists aren't honest and those

---

[38] *The Guardian* newspaper has recently published an article about prospective British tenants being asked to send a photo and personal information in order to secure a rental contract. Just like in Germany. Unsurprisingly, this is regarded as unjust and discriminatory by the Brits.
https://www.theguardian.com/money/2023/apr/09/landlords-demanding-renters-send-photo-cv-and-character-references

who are honest aren't perfectionists. One afternoon I had a viewing in a popular part of town and was excited about the flat, especially as from the outside the building looked like it wasn't falling apart. My excitement went up a further notch when I saw the flat even came with a kitchen sink and light bulbs. I noticed in the kitchen there was a fresh pot of what looked like green tea, but I didn't really give it that much attention. The flat belonged to the man's mother, who was elderly and frail and needed constant care, but she lived in a different part of town, or so the story goes. I liked the flat. The furniture, which I was told I could use, was old-fashioned and had a vintage edge, just the way I like it. He asked me if I had time for tea, and keen to make a good impression, I agreed. We had a nice chat about our favourite things to do in town and our love of independent cinemas for around thirty minutes over the tea he had prepared before I arrived, and then I politely said I really ought to be going. The arrangement we made was that I would see if I could get out of my flat early. If so, I could move into the new flat in six weeks. There was something, however, which made me reluctant about accepting so I got in touch with the landlord a few days later to see if I could bring a (male) friend for a second viewing and a second opinion. "No problem," he responded. But on the day of the second viewing, I got a message: "There's a problem and I might no longer be able to rent the flat. Please come to the flat and we can talk about it."

Not wanting to go alone, feeling something quite odd was going on, I asked if we could chat on the phone. The conversation confirmed my suspicions that something fishy was indeed going on. "You see," said the potential landlord, "my mother is very frail and she may pass away at any moment, in which case I'd have to move into the flat myself and therefore ask you to leave."

I responded with silence, so he continued, "And I've grown really attached to the furniture over the years and don't know if I'm ready to part with it."

"OK," I said, "it sounds like you're not really ready to rent the flat." He agreed.

Once it was established that a flat was no longer on the cards, I was ready to hang up, but he wasn't. "Maybe we could meet up anyway and go for a walk, or to the cinema," he said. "I've recently become single and I live alone," he added.

Suffice it to say my search ended with neither a flat nor an evening enjoying a French film. After an awkward and very disappointing ending I hung up and started my search all over again.

CHAPTER 22

§350 Ich mache es nicht, wenn es nicht gesetzlich vorgeschrieben ist

I won't do it if it's not prescribed by law

⤜⤛

As we have already learnt, Germans like being told what to do. This means they can't be blamed if something goes wrong. Moreover, rather than simply deal with fixing a problem if one occurs it makes far more sense to spend time berating Hermann for his mistake so that the naughty boy doesn't do it again. I once sent a parcel to another city in Germany but I got the postcode wrong. I also stupidly omitted to write my sender information on the back of the parcel; normally if you fail to do this you'll be reminded to do so by a clerk in a post office. I wondered why it took so long to reach its destination, until I was informed that when the sender information is missing and there is a mistake in the address, the German post goes away and researches the problem via an address research office. If there is a sender address provided, however, they'll send the letter or parcel back for them to correct. This makes perfect German sense as Hermann learns from his error and the German post saves the time and cost of researching the problem. My mother once accidentally wrote the address "*7 auf dem Steinen*" instead of "*auf dem Steinchen 7*" and the postman couldn't find the address and sent the £50 Christmas package back to England. There were ten houses on my street and my name was on the mailbox. Is it really that difficult to figure out who the intended recipient should have been?

On the subject of post, if you move to Germany and don't put your name on your letter box, expect not to receive post. This coming from a nation petrified of everything including paying with cash for fear of being spied on. For years my charming landlady Mrs Bouquet would make indirect digs at me as I hadn't printed my name on my letter box, even though on her letter box she had printed my name with an arrow pointing down the stairs so the postman could find my flat. That's assuming he could read, of course. I honestly thought a number, address and postcode would ensure my post reached me. You can go out full German style here and add your official title, be it, Dr or Prof. In Hermann's world, using your professional title is relevant at all times and places, except for perhaps at the workplace.

Common sense also goes out of the window if there is no law or rule to enforce it. Some time ago I was chatting to a neighbour who lives at *8 auf dem Steinen* when I commented that I found it somewhat strange that Germany hadn't passed a law requiring bike helmets. I really felt that this would be totally their cup of tea, but to my knowledge there was no such law in place. My neighbour, who won't wear a bike helmet but openly admits she should, nodded in agreement and said it was always better when there were strict laws passed and then you were forced to follow them. So, in other words she understood the importance of wearing a helmet and liked the idea of it being compulsory, but until then, she wasn't going to do anything, even though to her it made perfect sense.

Only in Germany

Nothing beats a nice bit of obsession over pointless details to add complications and meaninglessness to your life, and here the Germans are streets ahead, or perhaps even kilometres. It's just my personal theory that what Germans like to call "efficiency" is nothing other than getting bogged down in minor and pointless details. Germans just love gathering information for the sake of it; what you actually do with this information is neither here nor there. When I was offered a job teaching at a university one hour away by train from where I live, I went to the station to enquire about the monthly cost of a ticket between the two cities.

"How many kilometres is city X away from city Y?" asked the clerk.

"Uh?" I replied.

"Do you know the distance between the two cities in kilometres?" he repeated in a slightly more flustered and impatient tone.

"I'm afraid I've never really thought about it," I answered.

Seeing that I was truly stumped, the clerk went on to explain that he couldn't quote me a price as he couldn't see on his computer screen the number of kilometres between the two cities and this information was essential to calculate the price of my monthly ticket. Or perhaps an error of type 12,254 occurred. Or maybe Herr Schmidt was sick that day and he is the only person who can advise customers on distances between cities.

"Write an email or phone the *Deutsche Bahn* and ask them directly," was his final piece of advice.

Remember– when in Germany you always have to do other people's work, too.

Just for fun I once took a few beginners' language lessons in Japanese. During one of our classes the Japanese teacher provided us with a timetable of flights departing from and arriving in Tokyo. The goal of the exercise wasn't rocket science. We were to learn how to ask questions regarding travel in Japanese. A couple of minutes after the teacher had given out the handouts a young student put up her hand and asked, "Is this a real flight timetable?" Because clearly that was crucial information. I mean, how could you possibly practice asking for information such as, at what time does the flight leave, how long is the flight, etc, if the timetable is only pretend?

At university attention to trivial detail trumps, too. During a session outlining possible essay topics for a course, I asked if my students had anything they wanted to clarify before they got on with researching and drafting their essays. A timid hand went up. "How wide does the margin have to be?" was my only question. Once I'd recovered from the utter absurdity and pointlessness of the question, I told the student in no uncertain terms that I had never before considered the width of a margin and he needn't worry as I wasn't planning on getting a ruler out and measuring it. He looked rather confused but nonetheless satisfied with my answer.

In her book *Dear Oxbridge: Liebesbrief an England* (*Dear Oxbridge: Love Letter to England*), the German author Pollatschek outlines her incredibly frustrating experiences whilst studying at Oxbridge. Notably, the fact that in England, university lecturers don't measure margins and they focus instead on content rather than formatting.[39] I guess that must be hard to handle when coming from a country that marks exam answers as wrong if you put a tick instead of a cross in the right box.

German culture is in a nutshell so obsessed with rules and regulations that it's blind to pragmatic solutions even when these could produce vastly better outcomes. I'm not even going to mention that chaos that is Berlin airport. This lack of flexibility causes no end of headaches and surplus work for the average citizen. Fortunately, I managed to find a new flat in the end (with the help of a foundation that specialises in housing foreigners), and I wished to register my change of address with my vocational college. I was thus surprised to find out that my pay cheque, which I had specifically asked to be sent to my new address, was sent to my old one. The reason for this, I was told, was because I didn't provide an exact date of moving in on the form. Largely owing to the fact that my crystal ball was broken the day I filled in the form, I didn't know exactly when I'd be moving. Hence my change of address couldn't be registered. But it gets better. As if it isn't frustrating enough having to do everyone else's work because the average Hermann can't think beyond rules and refuses to do anything that's not in his contract, imagine when Hermann finds out he can't do what he needs to do precisely because of these very rules and regulations that *he* put in place. This happened at the start of the pandemic when, in the northern German state of Lower Saxony, the responsible authorities wanted to contact the elderly for the first Covid-19 vaccine. Due to their inflexible interpretation of data protection laws, only post office records could be used. But as the German post database doesn't always include a full date of birth, government officials had to guess whether or not "Fritz", "Ewald" or "Jana" sounded like an old person's name to increase the likelihood of reaching the relevant people. Nothing beats a bit of good old-fashioned German rigour, especially when it comes to combatting a worldwide pandemic.

---

[39] *Dear Oxbridge: Liebesbrief an England,* Nele Pollatschek, Kiepenheuer und Witsch, 2020.

CHAPTER 23

§563 Andere Länder, andere Sitten
Different countries, different customs

⤸⤳

The concept of punctuality also means something quite different to Hermann. Broadly speaking, if your class starts at 9 a.m., you should turn up to the classroom at 9 a.m. on the dot, whether a teacher or a pupil. After all, why be there a minute or two before you have to? It's your right after all to arrive just in the nick of time, even if insisting on your rights may inconvenience others. I once had a class conference at the vocational college at 1.30 p.m. on a Wednesday afternoon which was led by Herr Blockwart. At 1.26 p.m. I picked up my bag and left the staffroom, at 1.27 p.m. I arrived at the classroom. The door was closed and, being British, I knocked quietly and waited for a response before entering (I have been laughed at by Germans for doing this; the standard procedure here is to barge on in). When I entered, I saw Herr Blockwart standing alone in the middle of the empty classroom looking up at the clock. I tentatively asked if I could come in and take a seat, to which he responded by looking up at the clock again, looking back at me, taking a third look at the clock, then nodding his head to me, reluctantly. So, in I went, full of joy for what was to come.

I'll never forget the sense of panic I had though when I started doing English consulting for universities – I really thought no one was going to turn up. My seminars would always begin at 9 a.m. At least twice, after having travelled across Germany to an unknown city and having barely slept, I would arrive early to get the room and technology prepared – and at 8.58 a.m. I was still alone with absolutely no sign of life! My heart would start to beat loudly, I'd look at all the work I had likely prepared in vain, but then at 9 a.m., at 9.03

a.m. and 9.05 a.m., people would start to walk in, or rather barge on in. As just mentioned, knocking on doors and then waiting to be asked in will get you laughed at here. Learn to do it like a German – see a closed door, open it loudly and without a second's hesitation, and barge on in.

When seeing someone visibly struggle in the UK, for example, an elderly lady with lots of shopping bags or a small person with a suitcase roughly three-quarters their body weight, it's not uncommon to ask if they need help. We Brits, I believe, would see this as natural and logical. German sense seems somewhat twisted in this regard. Germans tend to shy away from doing this, largely as they don't want people to think they're going to steal something from the person struggling (as I learnt in a conversation course). Instead, it is expected here that if you want something you will speak up and ask for it. This is something that is encouraged in kids as soon as they enter kindergarten, because this is apparently what it means to be self-reliant and assertive, or so goes the logic. In Germany, it's the oppressed party who is expected to learn (what I call) the necessary "aggression" required to stand up for their rights. Until you learn this, you can only expect to be trampled on, stepped on, stared at, badgered, harassed, cut in front of and insulted. My neighbour who likes bike helmets but won't wear one told me about an incident at her kindergarten. Her very shy daughter approached a group of children playing in a group and wanted to join in, but the group shut her out. The teacher didn't intervene, her explanation being that if the child wants to join in, she must ask to play.

Similarly, whereas we tend to be rather too fond of the word "sorry" in the UK, I have heard from a fair few Germans that their equivalent, "*Entschuldigung*", may be seen as an admission that your behaviour is an imposition and by uttering this word, you're admitting that you're encroaching on someone else's comfort. It could therefore further explain why the word is used so sparingly. I have instead been encouraged to say a short and determined "*kann ich mal bitte*" ("may I please") – if possible and like a true German with a slightly bossy undertone – as it may create a different effect. Furthermore, in several encounters I knew with perfect clarity that if I wanted a certain person's help, I'd have to ask for it, loud and clear with a direct gaze and firm voice. I don't always have the surplus energy for this. Oftentimes the sheer physical effort I'll be expending can be less tiresome than the emotional effort of saying the right words in precisely the right way. It doesn't help matters trying to meet people in the middle and show consideration, either. The other day I was walking down some steps towards the bus station when I saw an elderly man coming my way but looking back over his shoulder. As I was already further to the left than he was, and closer to the handrail, I moved a little more in that direction so that he would be able to pass easily; particularly as he wasn't looking where he was going. As he comes within centimetres of me, he suddenly looks up, moves towards the handrail to block me off and condescendingly tells me that one should *always* pass on the right in Germany. Again, this you ought simply to know.

What I have come to learn from this is that apologising is often viewed as a sign of weakness and together with showing courtesy towards others it is bizarrely perceived as admitting some kind of intrusion on their private sphere. At least this is how the director at the vocational college put it. She finds it very strange if someone holds a door open for her, as it makes her think that this person a) isn't minding their own business (?!), and b) that she is not capable of opening the door herself. I personally don't rack my brain every time someone opens a door for me; rather I see it as a sign of consideration. But my boss put me straight – this is nothing other than an intrusion on her private sphere, as someone wants appreciation for something that they haven't asked for. I really am struggling to reconcile this strong defence of the private sphere and the amazingly intrusive German habit of telling every Hermann, Hans and Harold how to dress, cross the streets, clean their front path, and so forth.

This brings me on to the reputation of us "fake" Brits and Americans. I had one of my very few shouting arguments on this very topic (in contrast with their pushy behaviour, Germans shy away from direct confrontation. Indeed, Germans are both the fastest to seek a fight and the fastest to retreat). A friend of a friend once delighted in telling me that Brits like me don't realise that the question "how are you?", which we use far too often and without any sincerity at all, is hugely personal and when asked by a stranger, completely intrusive. She went on to elaborate, you'll be glad to hear.

Here's the logic: her injury, work crisis, lottery win, relationship break-up, etc. is not the business of a waiter, cashier, hairdresser, who is only there to *serve* her. Why, pray tell, when in a supermarket would that person actually care about my hip operation or my fight with my boss? It's not important how I feel, she proceeded to say, as long as we can perform an economic transaction. Somewhat blown away by this I let her know that you don't have to unload your whole life on someone in order to be honest. Moreover, you don't have to be friendly only towards the people with whom you have a relationship. Unfortunately, it turns out that my friend of a friend's view is more widespread than I thought – most Germans are able to be friendly with Hans who they have known since the age of five when they played in the sandpit together, but everyone else they can ram their shopping trolleys into.

CHAPTER 24

§318 *"Smalltalk" mit den Deutschen*
Small talk with Germans

⌒⌒⌒

Though socialising and friendly greetings, known in Germany as *"smalltalk"*, are too superficial and meaningless to engage in for the average German, it's not, oddly enough, meaningless to wish someone *"schönen Sonntag"* (have a nice Sunday), anywhere from noon onwards *on Saturday*; bark hello and goodbye automatically and robotically upon entering a room or a lift; bark *"guten Tag"* to your neighbour without smiling when you bump into them in the stairwell; bark *"Mahlzeit"* (enjoy your meal) to whomever may be tucking into a snack, and wish a customer lots of "fun" or "pleasure" with their new purchase. On numerous occasions after buying myself a new dress, lamp or pair of shoes, I've been told by the cashier *"viel Spaß damit!"* (have fun with it/enjoy) or *"viel Freude damit!"* (have lots of pleasure with it/enjoy). I'm always stumped when this happens. I find myself wondering whether this also happens when buying sex toys. I can imagine the scene; a couple go in to a sex shop on the hunt for a vibrator ... Let's just leave this idea there.

Other German small-talk topics, though no German will admit this, focus on the areas of: *"Magendarm"* (gastro-intestine issues) and *"Kreislaufzusammenbruch"* (circulatory collapse). My colleague at the vocational college, Ms Ticking-time-bomb, who went out of her way to avoid helping me and showing me the ropes insisted on being greeted in the morning and bid farewell at the end of the working day. As far as she was concerned, it was perfectly normal to look at me like something she had stepped on, scream at me for *looking* at her books in the staffroom, withhold important information from me, secretly monitor my hours, go through my desk, hide my exam papers the day before the resit pupils needed them, but my not saying goodbye at the end of the working day constituted the height of rudeness.

Only in Germany

One lovely organisation starting with "T" which I have already introduced you to has come up with a genius way of getting around this whole small-talk-I-have-to-be-friendly-and-polite-but-don't-know-how-to challenge. At the start of a meeting everybody is asked a set question, such as "Where did you spend your last holiday?" or "What is your favourite chocolate?" Participants must answer with one word. Further questions or elaborations are *"verboten"*.

Curiously, what also tends to be considered rude here is not saying your name when you answer the phone. In Germany it's customary to answer the phone by mechanically stating your surname. A woman who lives down the road – and who occasionally chats when she sees me – spent four months working in England. She told me that the rudest thing she has ever had to do, without question, was pick up the phone and say hello. She unfortunately couldn't draw the rather ironic parallel that she was actually being incredibly rude to her British neighbour simply by saying this. Seeing the look on my face, however, she did then hasten to mention that her husband only answers the phone with his name when he sees it's an official number from the city that's calling. I'm not sure that this is much better, mind.

In Germany it's safe to assume that you *should not* interfere when it's appropriate, i.e. whenever you see some element of danger or injustice, and you *should* interfere when you have absolutely no reason to. I suppose this makes sense in a country where dash cams are illegal. There was once a story in the local press of a lady who was fined for moving rubbish and glass out of the children's area to a safer space, as it was not her job.

A few years ago, I was excited to hear of plans for a new app in Germany where you could send photos of badly parked cars to the local police and gain 11 euros for the pleasure. I figured I could quit working for good and get rich quick if it ever came out on the market (sadly it never did). When I told a former university colleague, he looked at me stunned, mouth wide open, and said "denunciation". Yet it's perfectly acceptable to train kids in kindergarten to be "bin detectives" and give them a hotline to call if ever they see someone put their rubbish in the wrong bin. Similarly there's no problem in companies hiring detectives to check that their employees are working from home and not sunning themselves in the park; it's perfectly fine to be going out for coffee on a Sunday afternoon in high-heeled shoes only to be looked up and down and sarcastically told by a complete stranger that you have "great shoes for walking" (because all Germans from Bavaria to Berlin take long, aimless walks in the countryside on Sunday afternoons as it's *verboten* to do anything else). Likewise it's no problem for my neighbours who occasionally take my parcels to ask me why I have so many and what the contents are; it's 100 per cent understandable that my colleagues secretly monitor my hours in case I break the rules; and it's absolutely reasonable that when I book an appointment to see the doctor the receptionist asks me what for (even when others are in earshot).

For a long time, I struggled to comprehend how all these typical and everyday behaviours are *not* intrusive and *are* representative of "minding your own business", but, having worked in several schools here, I'm now slowly starting to cotton on.

CHAPTER 25

§416 Selbständkeit über alles!
Self-reliance above all else!

∽⌒∾

In Germany you can easily find yourself suddenly engaged in a theatre-of-the-absurd argument with a complete stranger and I have found that it helps if you are always on the defensive, or at least semi-prepared for potential combat. This is quite a challenge, mind. I often forget this and leave the house feeling perfectly content, somewhat in my own world, until I am rudely brought back to reality by a shopping trolley up my backside, or angry words from another fellow shopper who doesn't know how to use a divider on the conveyor belt and so ends up nearly paying for my goods. Anyway, one of my interpretations of Germans' tendency to steamroll others and tell people constantly how to behave thereby intruding on their lives is the sense of self-aggrandisement they derive from it. I really think part of the reason they behave like this is that they cannot handle the pressure of their own society. I have met many Germans who suffer from living in what they refer to as a typically German society. These have mostly been foreigners, my university students, or colleagues who have spent some time abroad and are yearning for more. In order to understand what I mean by this typically pressurised society and how it can bring about a tendency to be bossy and dominant, I'll start with the school system.

Germany requires twelve years of schooling, from age six to eighteen. Kindergartens do not belong to the school system and they have huge amounts of autonomy regarding how they instruct children. German kindergarten is the equivalent of preschool in America. Kids in Germany do not have to go there, it must be paid for, there is often no state curriculum and each one is free to set its own rules and didactic style. Kindergartens grant an extraordinary amount of autonomy to the youngest of children. Basically, kids are given free rein to run around and choose whatever activity they want to get involved in. Frequently the children don't even have to eat their meals together. My good old neighbour who won't wear a bike helmet but thinks it's a sensible idea told me that in her daughter's kindergarten the kids have regular "children's conferences" where the kids get together to complain and demand changes from the adults. Once her mother came to pick her up only to find her sitting alone in the corridor sobbing. When she asked the headteacher what the problem was, he just shrugged and said that sometimes we all need "alone time" like this. Occasionally there is some semblance of structure to the day, but it's heavily disguised as anarchy.

The necessity to speak up for yourself and thereby become "self-reliant" and "independent" (*Selbstbewusst* in German), starts as early as in the German "*Kita*" (nursery school). A key goal of the German kindergarten is the gradual ramping up of what's called "independence". Here, as just mentioned, the kids rule the roost; they can choose what projects they would like to do and interference and supervision from the staff is not encouraged. This is all part of the end goal of gaining "independence" and "self-reliance". There is also no punishment for any bad behaviour. Germans have completely rejected authoritarian ways of handling children. Corporal punishment, spanking, or hitting children by teachers or parents is against the law. One would be forgiven for thinking that this also extends to raising your voice to a child (at least judging by the times I have seen parents tell other parents, and complete strangers, off for disciplining little Hans in the street). You should instead treat your six-year-old child as a fully competent discussion and debating partner, your intellectual equivalent so to speak, and solicit their advice and opinion whenever possible. My neighbour – you know the one – well, she once recounted to me how she admirably dealt with that tricky topic of death with her daughter. Her kid came up to her one evening and somewhat out of the blue asked her where you go when you die. Her mother responded with "What do you think?" It wasn't her task to inform or educate her daughter you see; rather it was the mother's understanding that she should let her daughter's beliefs stand, no matter how bizarre or inappropriate.

Perhaps you're now asking yourself "What does a kid actually learn in kindergarten?" The answer is independence from parents, conflict resolution, and, most importantly, how to hold scissors and a pencil, and cut and draw neatly. It's not uncommon for parents to be told that their kid needs to repeat a year at kindergarten if they can't hold a pair of scissors or a pencil as they deem correct. *Remember – Germans have no real sense of order. They have a sense of symmetry. That is quite different.* As tidiness is next to godliness here, if a child can't cut in a straight line, colour within the lines, or has a chaotic exercise book, they can be told that they have to repeat the year. I can imagine a German adult would have a fit if they didn't manage to colour within the lines, even though they can't keep in their own lanes when driving. When he is not cutting, little Hermann will most likely be running around unsupervised and playing with his peers. Hermann even plays differently in Germany. It is not uncommon for kids' play to consist of kicking and pushing each other about. Oftentimes it escalates to picking on and bullying a particular child. Again, this very boisterous play goes on unsupervised and even bullying tends not to be taken seriously.

Only in Germany

This need to respect lines was wonderfully demonstrated during a trip to a local museum. It was a rainy Sunday afternoon so the new modern art exhibition drew in lots of visitors. In the first room there were a fair few people milling about. Standing at the back of the room was a short museum guard, with a curly moustache, who was watching, eyes like a hawk, an elderly man edging slightly too close to a painting. It made for awkward but addictive watching. The old man was getting ever so slightly closer to the work of art, the guard was edging ever so slightly forward too, head cocked to the side, like a wicketkeeper, ready to catch and stump the batsman out. And then it happened. The man overstepped the mark and put a foot in front of the white line guarding the painting. The museum guard bent down to a squatting position, knees out, eyes like saucers, and pointed to the white line. Not a single word was uttered.

CHAPTER 26

§288 Armutszeugnis Deutschland
Certificate of poverty Germany

༜

O nce they reach school age, there is a great amount of choice as to how and in which kind of school German pupils can study. A pupil (or more likely the pupil's teacher) can choose to pursue an academic or a vocational track. This choice starts very early on. By the end of primary school, the academic stakes get very high and pupils are put on to their future course by the tender age of ten; yet children have hardly realised emotional and mental maturity by that age. At ten years old children are placed on one of three paths: children who have wealthy parents who can afford all manner of private tuition and are thus automatically university-bound go to a *"Gymnasium"* (grammar school); pupils who don't get quite as good results are placed on a middle track and attend a *"Realschule"* (this can then lead to either university or a vocational programme). Finally, a third track, the *"Hauptschule"*, is reserved for those who wish to pursue a vocational education, or who have a foreign-sounding name. The *Hauptschule* has been now largely abolished, however. There are also *"Sonderschulen"* or schools for special education. It is largely the child's teacher who dictates where the pupil goes as they are given a recommendation for a particular school based on their grades, though parents do have some influence, too. Though it is possible to subsequently move between schools, the later the switch is made, the more difficult it is. Moreover, there is a fair amount of social stigma attached to the system, especially when a child is not recommended to a *Gymnasium*. I think you can imagine the human reaction of a parent upon hearing "your child is not suited for university studies". And as far as the child is concerned, isn't it rather traumatic to be told "you now need to decide whether you want to become an academic or pursue a trade?" The way I see it, the education system creates a ranking or caste system in which the roles are well defined. And in which people are put in their place very early on.

To further complicate matters in an already massively overly complex country, education in Germany is primarily the responsibility of each of the sixteen "*Länder*" or "federal states" and each and every state does things differently. Some states have centralised GCSE and A-level exams (or the equivalent thereof, "*mittlere Reife*" and "*Abitur*"), but most don't, and some states have an extremely rigorous and demanding system, such as Bavaria, whereas in others education is not so highly regarded, like in Bremen, for instance. To make things more confusing, some states have centralised GCSE exams but not centralised A-levels, some have centralised A-levels but not centralised GCSEs. And these centralised GCSEs are not in all subjects, just in German, English and Maths. Still with me? Each state has a different marking system and teachers who have completed their teacher training in Hamburg cannot teach in Bavaria. Though teachers have a ridiculous amount of freedom and independence if they teach in a state without centralised exams (I should know – I taught in one of them!), for the pupils the system is fairly rigid once a path has been chosen, or dictated. The chances for social mobility are not very high in Germany[40], and this system of separating children so early often locks their socio-economic status into place. It is a well-documented fact that a child's chance of success is highly correlated with parents' income and status, and children of immigrants do not do as well as middle-class German children. This can be clearly seen in some recent statistics. In 2020, 6 per cent of pupils left a *Hauptschule* without completing their education. Out of those pupils who had migrated to Germany, 15.1 per cent left without completing, but for those born in Germany with a migration background, only 3.9 per cent didn't finish their education.[41] This is not surprising

---

[40] *Achtung Baby: The German Art of Raising Self-Reliant Children*, Sara Zaske, Piaktus, 2018, p. 182.
[41] *Der Kita-Kollaps,* Wehrmann, p. 100.

information. The famous Pisa study back in 2001 revealed this. But since then, "*nichts*" (nothing) has been done. Furthermore, an Iglu study from mid-May 2022 revealed that around 15 per cent of primary-school-aged children hadn't reached the minimum standards in reading. Perhaps then it wouldn't hurt to learn some basics in pre-school? Maybe after dealing with all this it's no wonder that the typical adult is only too happy to avoid responsibility at all costs and let someone higher up make all their decisions for them.

Once in a secondary school, pupils are, broadly speaking, not encouraged to develop independent and critical thought. This is largely down to the fact that pupils are graded for *every* lesson, and as such it's much more important for Hermann to say what he thinks Herr Müller wants to hear. I was pretty gobsmacked when I once looked over at my colleague's desk at the vocational college to see a handwritten chart she had made with a grade and a percentage for every pupil's punctuality, oral participation and behaviour *per lesson* for the entire school term. The amount of numbers, charts and statistics was at first glance overwhelming, and I had to ask myself how much time and effort, especially during valuable lesson time, had gone into preparing this. She wasn't doing this for fun, either. In Germany, kids are graded for "oral participation", which means anything from whether you put your hand up during lessons, to how much you speak in class, to how tidy your exercise book is. Now I fully get that it's necessary for pupils to take part; I understand that it's important to be on time, but this is obsessive, overly regulated, and seriously detracts from teaching and learning time. Unsurprisingly, the degree to which oral participation counts towards a pupil's overall final mark varies from school to school (why be consistent here?), but where I taught it counted for a massive 50 per cent! I do wonder whether this is how many Germans become opinionated, pushy and dominant, feeling the need to add a pointless and offensive remark here, there and everywhere. Effective verbal communication is largely measured in terms of class participation, and the teachers I have worked with here are in favour of this system. Of course, it makes the teacher's job much easier when there are a couple of kids per class who are frequently willing to speak. As a result, subjects such as German, Modern Languages and History have frequently been termed "*Laberunterricht*" (waffle classes) by the kids, who see their role as taking over the class by leading fruitless discussions (a bit like on German talk shows) while the teacher can lean back, restricting their activity to the occasional intervention. Germans like and encourage this "laissez-faire" attitude of teachers as they argue that it helps children and teenagers learn that all important "self-reliance".

The importance of speaking up and participating goes even further, though, and pupils know it. Again, at the vocational college we have to dish out our participation grades to the pupils twice a term. The procedure goes as follows: the teacher takes the pupils out of the classroom one by one to have a brief chat about their oral participation grade and the reasons for giving them this mark (pupils must be informed of their grade and have the chance to question and debate it as an adult on equal footing with the teacher). Of course, it's not possible to teach while this is going on, so this lesson typically consists of pupils relaxing, watching videos on their phones and then pretending they've done the work you set them. But here's where the pupils have really got it good: if their grade, either for their academic achievement or for participation is low, they can increase it by giving an oral presentation or by handing in some voluntary work (the latter being much less common in my experience, mind). On the one hand, I can see how this is fair. Having been a very shy pupil myself, I would have leapt at the chance of handing in an extended essay to bump up my Science grade. Yet in many cases this simply allows lazy pupils to compensate for a term of doing absolutely nothing. I mean, if you can spend the best part of the term playing Candy Crush on your phone safe in the knowledge that you'll get a decent grade by doing a one-off ten-minute presentation at the end, why not try it?

It should come as no surprise then that the quiet, polite and shy kids get marked down, and the loud and obnoxious kids get better marks because of their "participation". This all depends on the individual teacher, who has too much freedom to make such decisions but invariably awards the higher marks to the noisy kids. I remember once when I was working at the private school, where King-of-the-desk is the deputy head, a pupil was being, in my opinion, quite aggressive and forceful with his opinions. I was giving my pupils feedback on their mock exams, when a pupil decided to take issue with the importance I attached to grammar[42] and show his anger quite visibly. When I asked him to calm down and reminded him that the classroom is not the place to argue and challenge a teacher's authority, he was very quick to tell me that he wasn't "arguing", he was "having a discussion" with me. And he is doing this because it will ultimately help him to get a better mark. It's pretty spectacular actually the sheer amount of disrespect that kids have for teachers, or adults in general, in Germany, all largely in the name of "personal rights" and the widespread mentality that it's my right to speak to you openly and aggressively.

---

[42] In Germany, children stop learning English grammar at the age of sixteen. The standard A-level programme at a *Gymnasium* does not have grammar teaching on the syllabus, as it is assumed that Germans have mastered all there is to know about English grammar by the ripe old age of sixteen. Fortunately, vocational colleges see things differently and grammar is still expected to be taught until the second of their third year of studies (at least in the state of North Rhine-Westphalia; I can't comment on the other states).

CHAPTER 27

§188 *"Quadrat, praktisch, gut"*[43]

Square, practical, good

❧

I stated earlier that anyone aged over forty has a slavish obedience to authority. Now I should mention that for anyone *under* forty it's best if their teacher, or anyone in a position of power to them for that matter, is dressed like a cool surfer who rolled out of bed just looking like that, so that we're all equal and there's no visible hierarchy. For we must all be the same. Germans have a deep hatred of anything that smacks of elitism, often criticising the English education system as a shining example, while failing to see that their own school system is blatantly elitist. The typical attire for a schoolteacher in winter in Germany is jeans, jumper and blazer; in summer, jeans, T-shirt and a blazer. You can perhaps add a piercing or a tattoo if you really want to be edgy. If you wear anything colourful, smart, or perhaps what we'd call appropriate to the situation, then you're just being "pretentious" I'm afraid.

I met a friend once after work, and as part of our ritual anecdote swapping (that's what tends to go on when Germans meet up with their friends for a drink), he excitedly told me about a book-reading by a French author he recently went to. What he found really cool about the evening was the fact that the author's hair was really messy and looked like it hadn't even been brushed; it was just "so *unpretentious*", to quote him. I have come to learn that clothing is not meant to express anything about you or your personality; on the

---

[43] This used to be the slogan for the famous *Ritter Sport* brand of chocolate. They've since swung to the other extreme with the slogan, *"bunte Vielfalt"* which translates as "colourful diversity".

contrary. It is meant to simply serve a basic function and be comfortable and practical for everyday necessities, such as eating, drinking, walking, sitting, telling off your neighbour, etc. The Germans really have taken the *Ritter Sport* slogan a little too far and have applied it to practically all areas of their life. Germans don't want to stand out from the crowd and draw attention to themselves and this is clearly shown in their clothing. It's not uncommon for couples to wear matching jackets, especially when out hiking, and as far as women are concerned, I think it's against the law to dress feminine. Barbara Vinken, a professor of literary studies who in 2014 published *Angezogen: Das Geheimnis der Mode* (*The Secret of Fashion*), wrote that even the way one dresses in Germany is an "aggressive act" as it sends out the message "I am fully functional, comfortable, don't need to impress anyone or be inauthentic and everything else I couldn't care about."[44] I think she nailed it.

So, when in Germany make sure to dress like a German and blend in. To begin, you can stick to the general rule that, "if it's there, use it". When in Germany you'll notice that most Germans use the strap on a rucksack around their chest, otherwise known as the sternum strap. Normally this is used if your bag is particularly heavy or if you're hiking a long distance, but Germans wear it around town as they've paid for it and it's there. Rule number two is that the scarf is not just for outside, it's for inside, at work, home, the opera, everywhere. You'll know if someone has a cold if they're wearing a scarf as, at the first sniffle, they'll break out some kind of huge scarf and keep it wrapped around them for days. Rule number three is that although colour is strictly *verboten*, it's acceptable to have colourful glasses that match the colour of your shoes. Credit where credit is due, the Germans do know a lot about funky glasses and they pull this off spectacularly well while managing to not look gay. Speaking of colour brings me on to rule number four. Once past the age of fifty, it's not uncommon for women to have a Liza Minnelli hairdo with a small stripe of purple, red or blue hair dye (but these are the only acceptable colours). Rule number five is that in Germany women look like men and men look like women. Lots of things changed in

---

[44] https://www.zeit.de/2013/39/rettung-barbara-vinken?utm_referrer=https%3A%2F%2Fwww.google.com%2F

various countries after the sexual revolution of 1968, and in Germany one thing that noticeably changed was the way in which (in particular) women dressed. German women wanted to speak up against the beauty craze through their clothes. High heels and skirts were seen as oppressive and pandering to male fantasies, so out with the fitted skirts and in with the shapeless unisex trousers. Whereas other countries, such as France, focused on things like women's contraceptive rights following the revolution of 1968, Germany got a little too fixated on the idea of clothes. At universities professors started dressing much more relaxed, pretty much like students, so as to eliminate the perception of this darned hierarchy. Typical clothes were an old pair of jeans or cords and a leather jacket. Women also donned these clothes and the gap between male and female started to close and to this day remains very much the same.[45]

Being a big fan of clothes myself, I thought it might be helpful and fun to provide you with a list of distinctive German attire. In order to stand a chance of fitting in and being unpretentious, you must obey the following rules:

- Trousers must always end around your ankles, with centimetres of sock visible not only when sitting.
- Your suit trousers don't have to match your jacket, but both ought to be shiny.
- Suits for men should be ill-fitting and preferably too short. Think Norman Wisdom.
- In cold weather, always wear an exaggeratedly large, thick jumper. Preferably hand-knitted but if you're not a dab hand at sewing then do your best to find a jumper that looks hand-made. This should be bright, multi-coloured and contain a distinctive pattern.
- In summer make sure your sandals are accompanied by thick, white tennis socks.
- Make sure your socks are always pulled right up. Even if they finish at that unflattering mid-shin height.
- Make sure your ankles are exposed all year round.
- Always wear brown shoes with black suits, and vice versa. If

you're feeling adventurous, throw in a pair of blue shoes to go with your brown suit.

- A rain jacket is never inappropriate (for Hermann must be prepared for *all* eventualities).
- For men, skinny jeans are always appropriate.
- For women, loose, unflattering jeans are the jeans of choice.
- For women, should you dare to break the rules and consider colourful clothing, blocks of primary colour, mainly on jumpers, are an acceptable exception. Remember here the *Ritter Sport* rule: "square, practical, good".
- For women, only wear figure-hugging clothes when pregnant.
- For men, pink, purple, mustard yellow, post-box red and green trousers are always a win.
- Rolltop rucksacks are all the rage and are never inappropriate.
- Alternative styles are invalid if not done properly.

In a nutshell then, in Germany you are not meant to be different or stand out. Imaginative Germans have even coined a wonderful word for those who neither follow the crowd nor bow to peer pressure; *"Muffel"*. The original meaning of this word is someone who is disinterested in or even against something. The most obvious thing that comes to mind here is *"Sportmuffel"*, which denotes someone who doesn't do sport or like sport. The suffix *muffel* can now be added to the most bizarre of words, heavily implying that if you don't go along with a trend, you deserve to be stigmatised for it. Only last week I read that many people in the state of Lower Saxony haven't cottoned on to the trend of heat pumps, hence they were referred to as *"Wärmepumpen-Muffel"* (people who don't want heat pumps).

If you have extreme wealth, you shouldn't show it (apart from with your car), if you have a dress sense that deviates from the norm, you're considered pretentious or a hippy if you demonstrate it. Yet kids are afforded massive amounts of freedom at nurseries, kindergartens and primary schools to explore and express themselves so as to become "independent", "self-reliant" and "assertive" human beings; teenagers can waffle away in class and get a good mark because of it, so what happens then to this sense of individuality and freedom later in life? How do we go from a society where kids dictate the rules, where teenagers are encouraged and expected to converse with their teachers and parents *as an equal*, to a heavily regimented and hierarchical system, as exemplified in school staffrooms, universities, and any dealings with civil servants, where adults are scared of their bosses, are bullied by their superiors *and* peers, and are constantly being reminded of their place? And what might all of this do to you, psychologically speaking?

Although German pupils experience freedom in terms of oral expression at schools, that's pretty much where it ends. Shy pupils are made to feel like there's something wrong with them as German schools want cookie-cutter kids who are in fact all supposed to be the same. When I was working at the private school the English teacher before me graded a pupil down in a test for using a perfectly adequate word. The word the pupil had chosen was actually much better than the one the teacher expected, but as the class hadn't learnt that word, the teacher marked it as wrong. So, in other words, the pupil was punished for being right. Independent thought was not rewarded. Come to think of it, independent thought would be so much more welcome at schools, but we've got a long way to go before that happens. A colleague at the vocational college told us in a meeting that several of his pupils had to ask him what name they should save their file under. They weren't able to think of this for themselves, perhaps by giving their file a title which was related to their project.

During one of our fortnightly conferences at the vocational college Herr Blockwart felt it necessary to share a story of his encounter with a "weird" pupil. It goes as follows: once when Herr Blockwart was on playground duty one of his pupils came up to him with a box of chocolates and asked if he would like one. Can you believe it? A pupil had the audacity to ask his teacher if he'd like a chocolate. Herr Blockwart asked us to keep an eye on this cheeky chap in lessons, since he was clearly exemplifying odd behaviour. I draw the conclusion from this that anything out of the ordinary, even or *especially* simple acts of kindness, is perceived as suspicious and needs to be put right, or punished, immediately. Anyone who departs from the principle of blatant self-interest is simply strange.

CHAPTER 28

§295 Achtung! Strafe!
Caution! Fine!

༒

The school system is in many ways a microcosm of society at large, and what never ceases to amaze me is the sheer number of rules governing how one is to behave in numerous situations, particularly in public. Let me name just a few examples off the top of my head: it is banned for adults to sit near or in public play areas designated for children at certain times (and largely flat-out *verboten* for kids over fourteen to hang out there); it is a criminal offence to take food out of a supermarket bin; it is forbidden to show someone the middle finger when driving; it can be a crime to insult someone in public[46], and it is forbidden to insult a civil servant (this being by far the most difficult rule not to break). This is a bit more than over the top, rather it feels to me like an act of needless intimidation by the state.

Poor Hermann can't really take anything for granted in Germany. The punishment for these "violations" is not proportional to the offence, either, and the police and *Ordnungsamt* in small towns and villages waste no time whatsoever in hunting down those who are doing all sorts of crazy stuff like sitting on the wrong bench at the wrong time of day. Now the worrying and even sinister thing with all this is the psychological connection between the extraordinary number of regulations and rules and the surliness and stiffness of Germans in day-to-day life. A pensioner in a conversation course even once hinted at this in a lesson about cultural differences. When

---

[46] You can find out more information here in this very illuminating article:
https://www.latimes.com/world/europe/la-fg-germany-insult-law-snap-story.html

talking about the lack of friendly greetings with neighbours and people you regularly bump into in supermarkets coupled with the tendency instead to robotically bark *"hallo"* stony-faced or laugh awkwardly and say *"danke"* (thank you) when asked "how are you?", she remarked that "Germans are just doing their best" as "this is their way of being polite". Indeed, I should "go easy on them" was her advice. Yet all this may go some way towards explaining why Germans don't tend to joke very easily, don't often smile, and are frequently cold towards those they don't know. I frequently ask myself whether somewhere at the back of their minds they may be aware that they don't have the same freedom to express themselves as people in other countries, notably English-speaking ones. After all, how can you ever be completely sure that you haven't violated one of the many random rules and regulations governing everyday life? If you do end up unintentionally putting a foot out of place, social disapproval won't be the only thing you have to deal with. Most likely you'll get a letter with a §, a hefty punishment and, worst-case scenario, a criminal record.

Typically German virtues (which are a myth anyway), such as the often-spouted efficiency, orderliness, thoroughness and punctuality are nothing other than the result of being constantly kept on your toes by a very heavy-handed and hierarchical system where people are always being reminded of and kept in their place, should you ever step out of line. And this line is only ever toed if Hermann thinks he might get caught, by the way. All these unnecessary rules must of course come with a (psychological) price, however. It helps account for why so many Germans can be so petty and love telling other people what to do and how to do it, since it means they can temporarily, or even momentarily, occupy a position of power. It helps explain their reputation as a nation of romantic brooders and deep thinkers who love nothing more than to while away the hours discussing and debating philosophical issues. Not infrequently have I heard that, unlike Hermann, the British do not like serious information with a lot of depth. As it turns out, the Brits much prefer reading the tabloids, so we must all be superficial. This is a theory corroborated by Annette Dittert, author of *London Calling: Als Deutsche auf der Brexit-Insel*. Dittert points out that "serious" newspapers like the *Financial Times* and *The Guardian* draw far fewer readers than the tabloids. Moreover, the Brits enjoy listening to radio stations which play songs back-to-back instead of stations which broadcast news. This can only mean that we don't care for balanced journalism or complex contents.[47] I wonder whether the Germans' self-professed propensity to think deeper thoughts, belong to a grand nation of "poets and thinkers", and critically engage themselves is a reflection of their punitive society, since if you're unhappy with and bitter about your flat/job/colleagues/low social standing/low pay/high taxes, you're more likely to brood on it, are you not? I would love to be able to walk down the street and not see people who want to bring me into line or put themselves out just to feel superior to me or report any minor thing which they perceive as incorrect.

A major cost of such micromanagement[48] in everyday life is often a rigid, pent-up, inflexible, miserable society, resulting in a population that is resentful, prickly, and suspicious of anybody who does things differently. Now of course, such people also exist in other countries – Germany is not the exception. But the damage that people can inflict here seems to be much greater and these people make up the majority, rather than the minority of the population. Whereas in many other countries you could generally just write off such people as a pain in the backside, in Germany you have to worry about them much more due to the chain-reaction of events they can unleash upon you if you're not prepared. Not to mention the Kafkaesque and expensive nightmares one wrong step can lead you in Germany. Take a former student of mine. Ever since he used his hoover one Sunday afternoon he has been constantly watched by his neighbour. Rather than try and deal with my student's bad behaviour by talking to him, the neighbour has taken it upon himself to call the police whenever he hears his son bouncing a ball indoors and whenever he invites friends over. In no time at all, the property management sent out a threatening letter with the symbol § informing my former student of his misdemeanour and the fact that

---

[47] *London Calling: Als Deutsche auf der Brexit-Insel,* Annette Dittert, Hoffmann und Campe Verlag GmbH, 2017.
[48] I'm sorry to have to say this, but society is just as micromanaged and overly regulated in matters of death.

he risked losing the tenancy on his flat if he continued. It seems that even the most minor report of behaviour that is incorrect is investigated immediately, vigorously and with great enthusiasm by the responsible authorities. The effect that this can have on Hermann's mental health is irrelevant.

For what it's worth, I think that's why there is so much emphasis placed on learning how to be "assertive" and "self-reliant" from the moment you're out of nappies. In reality, these words are nothing more than synonyms for "tough" and "hard". It also goes some way to explain why openly aggressive behaviour and the prevalence of "*schimpfen*" (scolding somebody) is simply seen as exercising your individual right for freedom. Since, the way I see and experience it, if you don't speak up for yourself, don't explicitly tell people what you need, don't push your own agenda through, you will not get anywhere and people will get away with bullying you. If in Germany a person is bullied, trampled on, ignored or shoved, you can't do anything but if someone says you swore at them without a witness, you're liable to receive a fine. What a mess! You need to treat life here as if in battle or in a jungle. Only the tough, robust and those with the pointiest elbows succeed; being independent or self-reliant, at least according to my understanding of these terms, has nothing to do with it.

CHAPTER 29

§778 Schämen Sie sich!
Be very ashamed!

❧

What do German dogs have in common with the average Hermann? You can spot a German dog a mile off, even though they're not typically decked out in tight three-quarter length trousers and socks pulled right up. Generally speaking, dogs behave just like their owners and show no interest in passers-by. The dog has somewhere to go, and only the destination matters. There's very little stopping and showing curiosity in strangers, hardly any fun-loving playing and sniffing and attempts to be stroked. Until recently, dogs were treated as objects in German law. Though this has slightly changed, dog owners' possessive attitudes remain the same. One must never show interest in a dog and try to stroke it, for the dogs, like German citizens, must know their place, and that's with their master. I was recently in the forest close to where I live and a beautiful black puppy slowly wandered up to me and I allowed myself to stroke it, half knowing I shouldn't. Its owner then promptly piped up, not directly to me, as although Hermann didn't want any direct confrontation, he wanted to be loud enough to be heard, and said to his dog "it looks like you have to go to dog school". When I went home, I checked out the legal status of dogs and came across this gem:

According to §90a BGB "Animals are not things and are protected by special laws. However, the same rules apply to animals that apply to things, unless the law provides otherwise."

I was relieved I had cleared that up. Dogs, like their owners, must be obedient and toe the line. In 2017 I went to the town of Emden to teach English to university staff. I stayed near a little park where there were many dog walkers. One morning, I saw something hanging from a tree. At first, I thought it might be little messages or gifts for strangers. Then I remembered I was in Germany. It didn't take me much longer to realise that, hanging up in a tree for all to see, were dog poos in bags. Check it out:

What you see is dog waste in a tree. As I said earlier, Germans can be very creative when it comes to showing people up and laying down the law, and the effort they put into petty acts of revenge really is second to none. A colleague explained the logic of the dog poo fairy to me: people had left their dog poo on the ground, hence hadn't fulfilled their civic duty, thus were deserving of this public shame. This seems to be the standard German equation and you'll be reminded of it whenever you happen to pass dog poo with a cocktail stick in it or see a bag hanging from a tree.

CHAPTER 30

§627 Geiz ist geil
Cheap is sexy

❧

This creativity of German spirit further extends to anything regarding money, or more precisely, when trying to avoid paying for something yourself. Should you happen to suddenly find yourself bored in a busy shopping street, try this game: drop a note from your wallet, with full hands, five times anywhere in Germany and five times in your own country. See how many times someone bends over to pick the note up to give it to you (once in a bakery I dropped a cent and it rolled and landed at the feet of the person standing behind me. He didn't budge). But Hermann will move mountains if it means <u>he</u> can save money. In Germany, the price is everything and the value is nothing.[49] Get as much money as possible, but pay as little as possible seems to be the prevailing attitude. What's more, it's perfectly acceptable to ask someone, even someone you don't know very well at all, how much they paid for their phone, holiday, rent, etc. and then tell them off for paying too much. The first time I had a friend over he spotted my Fairy washing-up liquid and, horrified, asked me why I spend so much on household goods. The lesson I hadn't learnt back then was that, when it comes to groceries and household equipment, you are only allowed to shop in discount supermarket chains. Brands are best reserved for clothes, rucksacks and footwear.

Germans pride themselves on the fact that they have so many *"Discounter"* or "discount chains". I'll give it to them; there is a wide choice of supermarkets, most of which are very reasonably priced.

---

[49] German schools are in need of 44 billion euros to repair them. The *Deutsche Bahn* needs around 60 billion euros to get it working.

There is no need to spend much on everyday essentials here and that does make a difference when things are tight. However, there is a downside to these *Discounter*. In what other country in the planet can you write "Poultry Salami" in big letters on the package and then have pork as the first ingredient? Where else do you get ground beef mixed with ground pork? This could be simply interpreted as proof of Germans' love of porkies, sorry, pork, but it has in my opinion more to do with their love of saving precious pennies (there is, after all, an eye-watering 1-euro difference between 100 per cent ground pork and a vile mixture of pork and beef).

In Germany it's not enough to just watch your pennies as closely as you observe Hans putting his rubbish in the wrong bin, you must also brag about your talent *not to spend*. In a pub one evening with a group of acquaintances the night was dominated by a guy's story of moving into a flat with no functioning shower. But at least it had a sink. Instead of getting one installed he decided to concoct one of his own, involving a bucket and a hose and some other stuff I didn't pay attention to. The evening was thus filled with joy, laughter and admiration for his penny-pinching.

Buffets also provide a wonderful opportunity for Germans to take advantage of the free food, steal some to take home with them, or be more obvious about it and come armed with a plate ready to stock up for the next day, and then boast about it afterwards over a beer. But I think what really took the biscuit (pun intended) was when a freshly qualified lawyer, who was tighter than a camel's derrière in a sandstorm, delighted in telling me how he managed to travel around the state of North Rhine-Westphalia on public transport *for free*. Clearly, he clearly had to count the pennies as a newly qualified lawyer, so he asked himself where he could cut corners, where he wouldn't have to part with his cash. And then the penny must have dropped (and been quickly picked up). The lawyer had gone and registered himself as a student in an obscure course of study at a university. He had no intention of actually following this study programme; he just wanted to bag himself a ticket allowing him to travel for free. As part of their semester contribution for their university degree, which amounts to a couple of hundred euros per semester unless you happen to find yourself in a semester where the fees have been temporarily abolished, all students in North

Rhine-Westphalia get a ticket allowing them to travel on regional transport throughout the whole state for free. They also get child support allowance and reduced entrance to museums, hairdressers, etc. Yet many still complain about studying being too expensive. This little trick is exploited by all and sundry. One of my friends is regularly teased by us as we often ask her how her studies in East Asian Art are going. She's a marketing executive. If you're coming to Germany and would like to pull this off, choose the most random field of study you can.

Only in Germany

Just like trying to get paid as a freelancer, or embarking on a game of musical chairs with *Deutsche Bahn*, a German divorce is not quick and easy. If both parties are in agreement, you need at least one year of separation first before you can start the divorce procedure. During this year of separation, you may share your living premises but must act as if the other person wasn't there. I'm not entirely sure how this is supposed to work. Possessions must be kept separate and if possible, not even in the same room. If both parties are not in agreement, then you must wait a minimum of three years before getting divorced. The average fee for a divorce is around 3,000 euros and the fees lawyers charge are based on the value of the divorce, so how much money or property you have. But this is something else that's perfectly *in Ordnung* in order and in no way constitutes too much intervention from the state, according to Hermann.

In 2015 the newspaper *Die Zeit* published an article with the title "How Germans tick". The last section of the article was devoted to the "sins" that Germans had confessed to committing. Four out of six examples were about Germans' propensity to cheat and lie in monetary matters.[50] Here are the results:

8 per cent confessed to lying on their tax returns.
14 per cent admitted to stealing goods for less than 5(!) euros.
6 per cent confessed to stealing goods for more than 5 euros.

---

[50] https://www.zeit.de/wissen/2015-08/deutschland-studie-wie-wir-deutschen-ticken-christoph-droesser

5 per cent admitted to not putting all their items on the conveyor belt.[51]

I find it rather illuminating that a) "sins" are measured largely in terms of honesty about money, and b) we're often talking about very little sums of money here. If you want to experience this fixation on money and penny-pinching first-hand, I strongly recommend going out for a meal or a drink with a German. When you ask for the bill, the waiter will ask you *"Zusammen oder getrennt?"* ("Together or separately?") This is always the first question asked, no exceptions. If you are ever out with a large group of people, be prepared to spend the last thirty minutes or so of the evening figuring out who owes what, down to the last penny. Bills are pretty much always split and the concept of buying a round of drinks doesn't exist, unless it's someone's birthday. This is another shining example of "German sense". You'll always know when it's somebody's birthday in Germany as on that day only they buy and take care of everything. A couple of times I've walked into the staffroom to see a table full of home-made cakes. The first time this happened I gathered that this was for someone's birthday, but what I didn't know was that the birthday boy buys or makes the goods for everyone, not the other way round. That's perhaps the only reason why I'm glad my birthday falls on 23 December.

---

[51] I think this is a very modest percentage.

CHAPTER 31

§327 Flexibilität und offenes Denken? Nee danke

Flexibility and open-mindedness? No ta

఼ఌఄ

Although money is perhaps the most important thing for Hermann, when it comes to applying for a job, he frequently has no idea what salary he'll get. In Germany, it is not typical for job adverts to state the salary. I didn't know what I'd be earning at the vocational college until the first day of my job. I awkwardly asked my director, who then proceeded to tap in some words to her computer and produce a sheet with various numbers ending with an "estimate" of my salary at the bottom. I had to wait until my first pay cheque to get the confirmation. For non-teaching jobs I believe Hermann has once again to show his "confidence" and "assertiveness" and state what he thinks he should earn, and then push his agenda through until the employer gives in.

This is not the only difference in the job market between Germany and the UK. In Germany CVs are expected to contain a photo and a date of birth. Occasionally, if you're particularly unlucky, an advert will state that fluent or even *"akzentfreies Deutsch"* (accent-free German) is a prerequisite. It used to be the case that CVs should also include your marital status, but I think this has been phased out. For a nation that is so obsessed with privacy and data protection I find this yet another glaring paradox, not to mention the fact that it clearly opens the door for discrimination. About halfway through my first two-year university contract, I started to apply for jobs and send out my CV to various other universities and companies. I very rarely got a response. When I mentioned my disappointment to a friend, he said it was all down to the fact that I didn't have a photo on my CV. "Go and get yourself a '*Bewerbungsfoto*' (application photo)," he forcefully said. Another nice little money spinner, I thought. Not only did I have to fork out the cash for an acceptable photo for my CV, I also needed to create an application portfolio for each and every job with all my certificates since secondary school graduation enclosed, which the company would then keep as they were too lazy and stingy to pay for the postage to send them back. I spent a tidy little sum sending out all those nice, glossy folders which I never saw again.

It's little wonder really that Germans expect to know your date of birth and what you look like. After all, age and image play a crucial role here and it's great to be able to categorise people so easily, think in small boxes, put people into boxes and judge them accordingly. At the age of thirty-five when I was having a sort-of-but-not-really interview with a university on the phone, I was amazed to hear the director happily draw the following conclusion: "and you're still young". What is one supposed to reply to that? And for a country that supposedly hates elitism (at least this is what they'll tell you), titles are regarded with extreme importance. Here's a little joke for you:

Knock, knock.
Who's there?
Dr.
Dr who?
Dr Dr.

No, that's not a typo. It's also not funny. But it is German. In Germany if you study for a doctorate degree and then do another doctorate you are referred to as "Dr Dr". And this coming from a nation who says they don't like to make small talk as all you do is state the obvious. In addition, if you hold the title of Professor in Germany then your official title is "Prof. Dr", as again, it's not obvious that in order to become a professor you have to have a doctorate. For Hermann, this must be specifically spelled out.

Remember – Germans have an exaggerated sense of personal status, both privately and at the workplace. It follows therefore that wives will refer to themselves as "*Frau Doktor*" (then name of husband), not just to tell the world that "my husband's got a PhD", but also in order to indicate that "I'm someone too." But what really and truly baffles me is that these extremely important titles aren't used as a matter of course in a professional context, so at your place of work (in my case, between university students and lecturers), but they are regularly used at the dentist's and doctor's. Apparently, it's no big deal if your students don't address you with your professional title, that's just stuffy and totally over the top, but heaven forbid your dentist omits your doctor title while billing you for your over-priced cleaning.

If ever you'd like to try your luck and apply for a job in Germany, it will help you to firstly know which one of their boxes you fit into and market yourself accordingly, and secondly, that here "*Vitamin B*" is indispensable. *Vitamin B* is not something you swallow as part of a balanced diet; rather it's the German for "important contacts". Even though there are now more opportunities for children from low-income families to land a decent job, they are still hampered by a lack of *Vitamin B* making it difficult for them to get a foot in the door. In my job at the private school, I kept on wondering why I was always getting files full of substantial errors by a colleague who was then swiftly promoted to head of department. It turns out that, though she was incompetent this didn't matter as her husband was working at an important ministry. However, I should mention that for some of my jobs in Germany I too have made use of *Vitamin B* (since it's pretty much impossible to get a job through the normal channels). I managed to get my second post at a university owing to a piece of chalk. I decided to attend a new colleague's lecture and when he went to write on the blackboard (the modern and high-tech state of schools and universities here is second to none. Mind you, I suppose that's better than being stuck in one of the more than 500 schools in North Rhine-Westphalia where the windows won't open), he realised he didn't have enough chalk. Being used to writing on blackboards myself I had a piece of chalk tucked away in my rucksack which I gave him. That was the ice-breaker which led to him putting me forward for another university position.

Once you have landed yourself a job, you should do everything in your power to stay there forever. In England, so the slogan goes, "A dog is for life not just for Christmas". Here, a job is for life. As my boss at the private school proudly announced to his sheep-like staff one day: "To make a big change tells the world you didn't get it right the first time." Germans tend to be extremely risk-averse and do not like change at all. Think back to "square, practical, good" – the German motto. If you do not fit into a box and fit the typical mould, you'll find it a real struggle here. Take my experience of applying for a flat. I had to phone up the landlady as she wouldn't accept emails. Her very first question to me was "How old are you?" Her second was "Why do you work in Cologne if you live in Bonn?" I wonder how these things are even relevant. But it all boils down to this: the mere idea that you happen to live in one city and work in another is too complex for the average German; it doesn't correlate with their idea of sense as it's not neat and simple; not *symmetrical*. And as it was such a tough concept for the woman to get her head around, I never heard from her again.

It's this obsession with titles and qualifications coupled with an irrational fear of change that is a major source of stagnation rather than success for Germany. A former student of mine from the US told me that for the two jobs she has so far had in Germany her bosses have had to give her false qualifications just to keep the HR departments happy. Whereas in the US or the UK, HR departments look at our qualifications AND experience and then deduce from what we have done so far whether we are capable of doing the new job, in Germany if you don't have the correct qualification or training to start with then you are pushed out from the beginning. In addition, all this "individuality" and "character" which you have supposedly been building up since kindergarten goes out of the window when you market yourself for jobs. Friends who have advised me on the interview process have told me to say that, if asked, my hobbies are sport and fitness. Again, if in doubt, think predictable and square.

What the Germans have done well in regards to studying and working, however, is create a varied and respected vocational track for those who wish to pursue a trade or do an apprenticeship. There is an astounding amount of well-developed vocational programmes available, and, importantly, those who choose this route instead of the traditional academic one are not as looked down upon as they perhaps are elsewhere. This surely goes some way to bolster

Hermann's important sense of self-confidence. But, as with most things, Germany has to overly regulate, take things too far and make complicated and unnecessary procedures out of what could be such a positive model for other countries. Working as a waiter for example requires a three-year apprenticeship, and even nowadays with the massive shortage of workers in this field, many owners of cafés and restaurants still seem to insist on this, at least that is what I glean when reading the numerous job adverts. Unlike in many other places, Hermann can't just leave school and take on some work to earn money, have some independence and gradually learn about the working world. No. Hermann must have a long-term plan! Though Germans like to point out that their system creates very knowledgeable and competent workers, what they fail to see is 1) should you ever wish to change careers later in life, the odds are so highly stacked against you as you're so specialised in one tiny field that you have little other choice but to stick it out in a job that you by now have come to despise, and 2) a considerable percentage of Germans don't stick out their training to begin with.

In 2016 one out of four apprentices in Germany dropped out of their vocational training programme, largely because they couldn't take the pressure. This mostly applied to manual trades such as carpentry, tiling and masonry. This doesn't bode well for a country with a shortage of skilled manual workers. Reasons cited for the high drop-out rate were firstly having to get out of bed early and secondly being too young, at seventeen, to have to go out into the world and carry out such demanding physical training. A further article from September 2023 pointed out that one in four apprentices also finished their training early. It's true that young people are required to be self-managers at an early age, be it in a trade or during a course of studies. When teenagers begin university in Germany, they are responsible for compiling their own timetable, making sure there are no course overlaps, and registering themselves online for all courses and exams. It's a big step up from school and therefore little wonder that 28 per cent of bachelor students quit their study programme. And for all the freedom of expression they have been used to during their school days, students here are reluctant to participate at all (note: university students do not get participation grades. I wonder if that has something to do with it). I remember once when I was teaching a German to English translation class, I thought it might be nice for the students to have some say in the materials we would be translating, especially after having seen that the department hadn't updated them since 1902. When I asked my students if they'd like to suggest translation topics I was met with silence. "You're the teacher," one student finally said.

CHAPTER 32

§175 Ich bin sehr leistungsorientiert!
I'm very performance-oriented!

కాహా

I quickly learnt that studying at a university in Germany provides the perfect opportunity to kick back, relax and fill your time with mini-jobs and travel. So why bother with an apprenticeship, eh? Whereas in the UK it's common to complete a degree within four years, in Germany you can take as long as you like. Though it's true that some students are super organised and work full-time while studying, this is quite rare. Just for fun I once asked some colleagues if they knew anyone who had been working on their bachelor's for a ridiculously long time. The winner was a student in the department of Archaeology who was in his 100th semester. He was probably so fascinated by ruins he wanted to become one himself.

A couple of times I've embarrassed myself by bumping into former students in town many years after I stopped teaching them, asking them what they're up to now only for them to say, somewhat awkwardly, they're still working on their bachelor's. Students you must understand have it pretty cushy. Figures reveal that 43 per cent of young adults live at home with their parents.[52] Though it's becoming more common for German teenagers to fly the nest and move out of home for their studies, it's still relatively rare. Parents are also legally required to pay for their children for the duration of their studies or up until the age of twenty-five. Only when they are working and fully self-sufficient do they have to pay their own way.[53] But the real incentive for staying at university until you're an OAP, as

---

[52] *Achtung Baby*, Zaske, p. 178.
[53] *Achtung Baby*, Zaske, p. 183.

far as I can see it (apart from that very handy reduced transport pass of course), is health insurance. For many Germans, especially freelancers and the self-employed who need to take out a mortgage to cover the costs of their health insurance, students have got it great. Up until the age of thirty they can enter the public health insurance and get a "cheap" rate for around 70 to 80 euros a month. Students older than thirty are still eligible, but they have to pay more, roughly 170 euros per month, hence the same as a low or *no-income citizen* (!). That's why it's not unusual for Hermann to finish his studies at thirty. Though it does make you wonder how being aged fifty makes you too old for the job market if you've only entered the working world at thirty ... yet another glaring paradox. To fit in like a true German, I suggest staying in education until you're in your thirties and then start acting like you're still in kindergarten when you finally enter the workplace.

As *The Economist* magazine recently pointed out, Germany is great at scoring own goals and should perhaps be referred to as world champions in this field.[54] Like many countries, Germany is and has been suffering from a severe lack of skilled workers in manual fields for a long time now. We are in desperate need of manual labourers, kindergarten teachers, electricians, and nurses. Yet university lecture halls have been overflowing for years, with students sitting in the aisles and waiting a semester or more for a spot in a course. So what has Germany decided to do about these twin ills? Ignore them completely and create a programme called "uni on top" which provides the most successful A-level pupils who pursue commercial professions the opportunity to study a semester or two alongside their apprenticeship at a university. What's more, the subject they get to study is already the most popular university subject in Germany "*Betriebswirtschaftslehre*" (business economics); the subject that allows people to bag themselves high posts in management. Some universities (Duisburg-Essen, Düsseldorf) are now actively seeking out students as far fewer people enrolled in German universities at

---

[54] Is Germany once again the sick man of Europe? https://www.economist.com/leaders/2023/08/17/is-germany-once-again-the-sick-man-of-europe?utm_medium=social-media.content.np&utm_source=twitter&utm_campaign=editorial-social&utm_content=discovery.content.evergreen&s=08

the start of 2023. I ask myself how this is beneficial for the economy when we have such a shortage of manual workers <u>and</u> when universities have been overcrowded for decades. I strongly feel it's just another German own goal in the making, together with their talent for acting on a whim and making knee-jerk reactions.

Only in Germany

For a nation that puts such a high price on having the proper qualifications and the proper piece of paper, it would be nice as an employee to have these standards matched and occasionally have a proper work environment. Several times I've been virtually unable to carry out my job due to a lack of working facilities. At one of the more prestigious universities I worked at, there was no Microsoft Word on my computer, only WordPad, despite an IT expert having looked into the problem. I was also unable to save paper and use an overhead projector as they hadn't been working for weeks. And due to a technical glitch in the online system, which took as long to fix as it took Berlin airport to be built, I had to manually register each of my students one by one to the server. Naturally I was frustrated, so figured I'd report the issues with a hope of getting support. Here was my answer:

> *Dear Dr Dunn,*
>
> *regarding[55] the OHP and all OHPs ... The university does not offer any support to keep them in a good state of repair. The department will have to bear the costs and refused to do so in the past. A portable OHP is available, though.*

That was the sympathetic part of the message. That money was not to be spent on tools to enable me to carry out a job was meant to be understood as a given. Shortly after I had to be put in line for having had the audacity to question the state of equipment:

> *Regarding the copy costs: 2,000 copies <u>per year (no copies for</u>*

---

[55] Emails in German begin with a small first letter. This is because it follows a comma, and after a comma one uses a small letter, silly.

students!!! ... they will have to copy samples at the library desk!) will comply with the 5,000 Euros budget per year for the entire staff of the English department. More copy costs will be at the expense of all other budgets, including the professors' budgets._

And the final sting:

Always use your uni-xxxxx address and not your personal address!!!

It didn't matter that my university address didn't work. As we have now come to learn, the issue had to be turned around on to me. I often fantasise about what it would be like to be treated with respect and appreciation, hell, even a modicum of dignity would be nice.

Though I enjoyed watching the Chuckle Brothers as a teenager I didn't expect my life as a university employee and schoolteacher in Germany, with all its failures, flops, stilted conversations, arbitrary scenarios, incomprehensible rules and lack of professionalism to bear such an uncanny resemblance to it. Yet I'm sorry to say it gets worse. Working as a freelancer taught me just how much this place is random with a lottery-like approach to most things and is intent on finding fault with the little man. But it also gave me a huge and important insight as to why poor Hermann stays put in a job for life that makes him a miserable, pent-up robot just waiting for his next opportunity to lash out at the next innocent bystander.

CHAPTER 33

§439 Courage ist gut, aber Ausdauer ist besser

Courage is good, perseverance is better

❧

Germany's system of solidarity is very strong and its citizens are covered in states of fragility. Sound familiar? I've lost count of the number of times Germany has been hailed as a fair and equal society. I think what people must have forgotten to mention here is that, as I've been told in no uncertain terms several times, if you cannot afford to pay your health insurance, you have no place to be here in Germany. In Germany, a freelancer or self-employed person is solely responsible for forking out their monthly health insurance payments themselves, whereas if you are employed you share the costs 50/50 with your employer. Moreover, if you are employed you get a pension and nursing home insurance. You pay both of these yourself if self-employed, and yes, you are legally obliged to do so.[56] And something I only recently learnt was that working freelance makes me ineligible for unemployment money if ever I lose my job. Even though I am paying taxes here. Freelance language teachers in Germany are effectively on zero-hour contracts but their situation is worse than elsewhere because of the compulsory monthly health insurance and pension payments. In case you haven't already noticed, Germany doesn't reward innovation and going it alone, which partly explains why the country has so few start-ups. This 50/50 deal is obviously much more lucrative for the average

---

[56] Many professions are exempt from paying their own pension as a freelancer, but teaching isn't one of them.

Hermann, and those who wish to strike out alone are usually stopped before they have even started.

The German system does not favour low income or self-employment. Unless you are consistently generating a substantial profit, stay the hell out of here would be my two cents' worth. Unsurprisingly, the system also provides many hurdles for low and middle-income self-employed workers and the paperwork is difficult even for most Germans, let alone for foreigners without a fluent command of the language. In order to understand the multiple regulations involved, foreigners will need to hire expensive professionals to complete their everyday tasks for them. Remember those handy "Income Tax Help Associations" I told you about, that place you can go to in order to get assistance filling out your yearly tax returns? Well, these aren't an option for freelancers and the self-employed; they're left stranded. They're supposed to get an independent tax advisor (of which there are 90,000 in Germany. Just compare that to France where there are 20,000; it tells you all you need to know). So coupled with the extra costs of insurances that the self-employed have to pay they are also barred from getting affordable assistance with their tax returns.

When I told this to my students in an intensive Business class, even they were shocked. No one realised that my freelance status made me ineligible for free or even reasonably priced tax advice. This revelation got them talking about their own experiences dealing with their tax returns. One student told us that she gets more money back than her partner for her home office; even though they live in the same house and use the same office. They don't want to raise this with the tax office though as it would most likely mean losing even more money. The German tax office seems to have a sort of license to extract any amount of money they dream up, whenever they want and for whatever reason. One student told us that she had taken her tax office to court as they accused her of hiding money in her home country of Italy. As she's also a language teacher, and *not* a civil servant, I doubt she has two cents to rub together. Another student (so the third out of a group of five), told us that she had to redo at least two wrong calculations on her tax return last year. And then plead with the tax office for months until they finally admitted their mistake and reimbursed her. *Remember: "Ausdauer ist besser", perseverance is better* (than courage), as the author Theodor Fontane once wrote.

Let's now take a look at some well-thought-out, rational and fair German figures. After all, this country is well known for its rationality, fairness, and order. German health insurance companies are by law obliged to *ignore* your low income and charge you as if you had made a certain minimum amount a month. Hence, they concocted a *fictitious income* to make their lives easier and screw over the self-employed. Up until 2019, this fictitious income was calculated as a shockingly precise and high 2,283.75 euros a month, so Hermann would pay as if he were earning this sum, even if he had earned 800 or 400 euros. So that's a hefty 320 euros a month health insurance thank you very much! This morally criminal law was changed at the start of 2019. Having finally realised that very few freelancers make this kind of money, the fictitious income was lowered in one fell swoop by more than half (!) to make a new fictitious income of 1,061.69 euros. Now if freelancers earn *less than* this amount, they still pay as if they had earned this, and their contributions come to about 160.54 euros a month. Add on to this 35.04 euros for compulsory nursing care insurance, or more if you don't have children. After rent, pension contributions and compulsory TV tax (which you must pay even if you do not own a TV and are deaf and blind), you're still barely able to make ends meet though. Just bear in mind that freelancers in certain fields are legally required to pay pension contributions of 18.6 per cent per month (this comes from a 1913 law that mandates freelance midwives, fishermen and teachers need to pay into the social security system). This is particularly disgraceful when you take into account that Germans receive less than 50 per cent, somewhere around 48 per cent to be precise, of their gross salary for their pension. The other two options freelancers have is that their income is flat-out ignored (just like it used to be for health insurance) and they pay either half of the regular contribution at 305.97 euros a month or the eye-watering full contribution at 611.94 euros a month. Much better to stick with that hateful makes-me-sick-but-gives-me-a-liveable-salary job.

Only in Germany

While we're on the topic of making stuff up and playing around with numbers to screw over the average Hans and make a quick buck, did you know that several Covid test centres across Germany have been lying about the number of tests they've been carrying out? It's recently been discovered that one in four of the 2,400 test centres in Berlin alone claimed to have carried out far more tests than they actually did. On 13 May 2022 somewhere in the state of North Rhine-Westphalia, WDR, a public radio and public television broadcaster in Cologne, and NDR, the state broadcasting corporation for Northern Germany, counted the number of visitors who came into a test centre. According to their reports, fifty-two pedestrians and 101 passengers in cars came to be tested. So how many tests did the centre report for that day? 2,670. In a country where you need to undertake a course and get a licence to play golf, you'd think that the authorities would be able to control how many tests were being conducted during a global pandemic.

CHAPTER 34

§277 Augen zu und durch!
Grit your teeth and get to it!

∽⌒∾

As mentioned earlier, after having experienced purgatory – working life with a contract and part freelancer – I thought I might as well go all the way to hell and test out Germany as someone who's 100-per-cent freelance. It was never a choice, but over time I got pushed more and more in that direction. Since becoming 100-per-cent freelance in August 2021, I spent the best part of four months trying to sort out my monthly contributions with my health insurance provider. The monthly rate now seems to be fixed – unsurprisingly it increased again by 8 euros this year. It took about the same amount of time, but a lot more paperwork, to find out how much pension I'd have to pay every month. They required an estimation of my salary. This is all fine and well in theory, but when you're working freelance income generally tends to fluctuate, particularly when you're just starting out. So, after doing a lot of sums I figured I'd be earning around 1,060 euros a month for around fifteen hours of teaching per week. Based on that (very modest) sum, my pension provider demanded a monthly contribution of 190 euros, and my health insurance provider 224 euros. As difficult as it is to admit, I'd be financially better off unemployed. I mean, I'd be earning around 12,804 euros a year; in 2022. After expenses that leaves me with just about enough money to live for, say, forty-five minutes. And the final kick in the teeth as you know is that I won't get unemployment benefits if I lose my work.

These little freelancers who earn peanuts but fork out tons are easy prey for German authorities, who are continually coming up with yet even more imaginative ways to screw them over. One of my friends has had the balls to go it alone and has set up her own modest business as a goldsmith. Respect. But as you can't swing your own dick in your bathroom in Germany without hitting upon a law or getting punished (not that I've ever tried), she was in bits when she received a strongly worded warning from a dubious organisation who fined her 3,000 euros as, according to them, her website contained a "controversial statement which needed to be deleted". Seeking solace in another of her self-employed friends, she twigged that something, unsurprisingly, very criminal was going on with search engines targeting small business owners. Her friend who sells scarves online had also received a warning and a threat of a fine of 1,500 euros as she had misspelt a name and forgotten a comma. If she didn't immediately rectify this, she'd have to hand over her hard-earned cash.

Indeed, the German population seems to have a real feeling of hatred towards freelancers and the self-employed. It's not just the authorities who are after us but people at large. To paraphrase a prevalent German logic, the self-employed are selfish as they go off and do their own thing, are not part of a community and hence do not act out of "solidarity". At the very extreme end of the spectrum, us freelancers are hippies.

I am, therefore, left with the distinct feeling that the daily unscrupulousness that constitutes life in Germany is that bit stronger for the self-employed. With this realisation I accepted a contract at the vocational college in 2018. Luckily, I only worked there for "39 per cent" of my time (as it was stipulated in my contract). For the remaining 61 per cent of my time, I worked freelance. This I filled up with teaching English to adults in various organisations and schools. Though in no way a bed of roses, my freelance work does offer me a much-needed respite from the back-stabbing and bullying of my contracted jobs. It has actually stopped me from going insane. I've had the good fortune to meet many intelligent and open-minded students, who have also taught me a fair number of things or made me see things from a totally new perspective. The icing on the cake, though, has been the sheer kindness of several of my students. At the start of the Covid pandemic in April 2020 my courses at one of my places of work had to be cancelled. The students were given a refund and three of my students offered to pay their reimbursed course fees into my account. I was extremely touched by this and will never forget the generosity of this gesture. What's great about teaching English here is that you can frequently meet people who take an interest in you as a human being, who are keen to engage in interesting topics of conversation, who enjoy digging deeper and bringing something new to the table. Some of these exchanges have proved so enriching, funny, memorable, or all of the above that I've gone on to develop some lasting friendships with several former and current students. I would go as far as to say that it's my students and my rewarding interactions while teaching that have kept me here in Germany.

A case in point here is a lady who was in one of my English for Work courses. She was always lively and active, and even attended class when she was suffering from a Covid infection (the lesson was online, but still ...). From the start it was clear that she was getting a lot from the course, so towards the end of the semester she asked me if I'd be interested in giving her private lessons focusing on how to conduct career interviews with university students in English. Naturally I jumped at the offer. Without further ado she spoke to her boss at the University Careers Centre and they agreed to start straight away. Not all the official channels had been gone through, but as my student sung my praises, they made an exception on my behalf. No sooner had I started teaching than my student kindly pointed out that my hourly fee was too modest and I really ought to be charging more. She encouraged me to sell myself, to highlight my experience, and even formulated something in German for me to say. Thanks to her, I managed to increase my hourly fee by 15 euros in one fell swoop. Since then, she has continued to "sell" me to various colleagues and institutions and get in touch when she sees a job offer that might be of interest to me. Meeting such kind-hearted people goes a long way and certainly offsets the pettiness and stresses of everyday life.

My life as a freelance teacher didn't get off to an altogether smooth start, however. A couple of times a student refused to answer a question, or gave such an inappropriately honest and personal response that I was at a loss as to how to continue, just like the time a student told us that she once missed a flight as she was having sex with her husband. A student once refused to say, for example, what had been one of her greatest accomplishments, as she considered the question too vain (she could have made something up), and to the question "what challenges have you overcome?" posed during the introductory session of a Business English class, a participant answered that they once recovered from a life-threatening illness. Now I was touched to hear this, but for what I considered rather standard questions I was also gobsmacked by the nature of the answers I was getting. *Remember – Germans can't do context.* At least not immediately, anyway. The following week one of the participants said during class that they had been thinking all week about why they gave such a personal answer and they realised only much later that they could have chosen a number of other banal things to recount. I, for my part, learnt to tone down my questions for the German mindset in the future!

In early 2021 I came to learn first-hand the meaning of a few key German terms. Working without the security of a contract in a country that largely feels that freelance teachers are a waste of time gave me a valuable insight into the much-lauded spirit of "*Ausdauer*", "perseverance". This coupled with dealing with bureaucracy to get my residence permit following Brexit at the start of 2021 taught me the real meaning of "*Augen zu und durch*", "grit your teeth and get to it". On a chilly May morning at 9 a.m. I had an appointment to pick up my permit. Being on a Monday, I really needed this appointment to run on time so I'd make it back home in time for my marathon online teaching session. When I made it to the venue, I was greeted by a bunch of individuals staring aimlessly at their phones in front of a big, iron black gate. I knew I was in the right place then at least. Suddenly it's 9.10 a.m. and my name still hasn't been called. I start to feel a bit restless and on edge. At 9.20 I think I hear someone shout out the name "Louise Abigail Dunn", so I walk up to the gate wondering whether they called me Louise, my middle name, earlier and I didn't react. A middle-aged woman, hair as spiky as her greeting, demands to see my letter and negative Covid test.

"I don't have a Covid test; the letter doesn't mention it," I plead, waving the letter in front of her. As soon as I do this, I start to see nods of encouragement from others in the crowd. No doubt they'd been through this too.

"The rules changed about a month ago due to the rising number of infections. You now need proof of a negative test to enter the building." After a slight pause, spiky Frau Siebert continues, "There's no point in looking at me like that, Frau Dünn. We don't make the rules."

Experience has taught me that there's about as much point trying to reason with government officials as there is expecting to get from Cologne to Bonn on a German train on time. I had no choice but to find there and then a place to get a test with an immediate result. Luck was on my side and, just a five-minute walk away, I found a test centre with no queue. The man at the desk understands my predicament as he's had foreigners coming through all morning requesting a test for their permits. Without so much as a sneeze or a retch I do my test and wait for the results which are sent to me via email as a PDF. But there was the snag. Whenever I step foot outside my flat, my internet connection is shaky at best. I was unable to receive the email with my test result. When I mention this to the staff I'm told that this is a zone with a "*Funkloch*", a lovely German word for a "black hole".

Feeling even more on edge than I did before my middle name was called out, I trudge back to the foreigner's office whereupon I see a young man arguing with a civil servant about the fact that his letter didn't specify that he needed a negative Covid test. I figured that if I helped him out and directed him to a test centre, he might help me out in return and let me use his internet connection. My plan worked like a charm. When his test was over, the queue had grown to resemble a German queue for ice creams, in other words it was massive, so we decided to grab a bite to eat. We'd well and truly missed our appointment slots by that point anyway. We grab ourselves a take-out coffee and keep on checking back with spiky Frau Siebert and company, but we are repeatedly told "*Nein!*" I carry on chatting with the helpful Brit who's letting me use his internet when the heavens open. I try to put my coffee down and open my umbrella, but instead I drop my coffee and it splashes up on his shoes and trousers. I wanted the ground to swallow me up. This young man had been so kind and patient, and I'd just messed up his clothes. He assured me it was no problem and his shoes were old anyway. But still, I felt pretty humiliated. At 11 a.m., two hours later than originally scheduled, I get called in for my appointment. I walk in to see a youngish woman wearing a shirt with the sort of pattern you get when you rub your eyes too hard, green and red glasses and strong perfume sitting at her desk growling at me. In any other country on the planet this might make for an unusual combination.

"Frau Dünn, you need to be on time for your appointments," was my greeting.

I couldn't be bothered to protest so I let her get on with her document checking, just hoping to get out of there as quickly as possible. She sends me off to a machine where I can do finger scans and get a photo for my residence card, but as my fingers are frozen it takes some time for my scans to be accepted. I'm almost done when the woman comes in to check on me, or hurry me up, as I'm obviously keeping her waiting again. As soon as everything's done, I make my way back down the hall to her desk.

"I'm done with—"

"No. You're not finished," she interrupts. "We still have procedures to go through."

What I wanted to say was that I was done with *the machine*, not with our meeting. But I didn't get that far. I sit with her for at least another ten minutes while she shuffles through various bits of paper, coughs and goes to great lengths not to meet my eyes. When she's had enough of that I'm told that in about six weeks my residency permit will be ready and I'll have to come back to collect it. The prospect fills me with no end of joy.

Only in Germany

To a certain degree it would appear that being a judge in Germany is somewhat akin to being a teacher. In German courts, only formalities are written down (what someone was wearing, their age, behaviour, etc.) and criminal cases are not recorded. There is no audio document, no transcript. *Nichts.* So a decision is made on what the judge jots down on their A4 paper in court.[57] Another classic example of German hard work and rigour.

---

[57] https://www.sueddeutsche.de/panorama/prozesse-justiz-video-aufzeichnung-1.4497281

CHAPTER 35

§208 Weltmeister Spaß!
World champions in fun!

⤬⤬⤬

So how does Hermann like to relax after a hard day of berating people for the most minor of things? Well, another benefit of teaching English is the insights it has given me into how Germans like to spend their free time. I feel you can learn a lot about a person by the way they choose to spend their time when they're not working. Broadly speaking in Germany, hobbies are: sports and shit-slinging in the direction of your neighbours. Having a barbecue with the friends you made in kindergarten is also a socially acceptable way to spend every sunny evening of the year. I mean, Germans really are diverse with their hobbies. Be it basketball, tennis, cycling, jogging, or even all four! You name it. Variety really is the spice of life here. And remember: when you take up a new hobby make sure you do it to death. In Germany, sports are not just perceived as something fun and a way to wind down after work. No, sports are also all about discipline, duty and "toughening yourself up". OK, there are also some other really exciting things Germans do in their spare time. These include: going on bike tours (seemingly the most popular type of sport here), playing board games, dressing up and doing fantasy role-plays and, most excitingly of all, getting a beer from a kiosk and chilling by your local river or lake with someone in the twenty-seven to thirty-eight age-range. It is imperative that your friends are not much older or younger than you, otherwise how can you possibly have things in common? Ideally, hobbies should be conducted in a "*Verein*" or club. At least 15,000 new clubs are formed a year.[58] It's

---

[58] *Leben in Deutschland: Anatomie einer Nation. Ein ZEIT-Buch*, Theo Sommer, Kiepenheuer und Witsch, 2004, p. 200.

great to be a member of a club with its hierarchies, sense of discipline and order. According to German logic, clubs are an important contribution towards "social integration" and are evidence of a "democratic society". In my humble opinion, Germans need clubs as they are too uptight and incapable of starting spontaneous, friendly chats with people in everyday life and finding out that they have things in common, so they need to go somewhere where all this hard work is done for them. Nearly everyone in Germany is a member of a club and if you look, you'll find there's a club for pretty much everything under the sun. Clubs are good for Hermann because their meetings happen the same day and time every week or fortnight, thus providing him with a stable routine and warm refuge after his hard day at the office being spat on by his colleagues.

Spontaneous fun doesn't exist in Germany. Their famous carnival celebrations which take place in February are organised from 11 November. From this date onwards weekly carnival meetings take place in one of many carnival clubs, ensuring that the three days of carnival "madness" and letting your hair down are as predictable as possible. After all, Hermann must occasionally enjoy himself, and he is performing a duty now. Though Germans love decking out from head to toe in their expensive Nordic walking attire for a brief stroll in the park, the outfit of choice for carnival is a highly unimaginative tiger or lion onesie. Failing that a hat will do. Halloween is also celebrated in Germany, though here it's called "*HELL-o-een*". I guess Halloween did prove rather hellish for my lovely former landlady last year. I came home one evening just after Halloween to see her cleaning her door bell. I know Germans must have a spotless home so Herr and Frau Müller with whom they've been neighbours for years cannot judge them if they have a speck of dust in the corner of their living room, but I thought this was taking things a bit far even by German standards. Upon closer inspection I discovered that she was cleaning ketchup off her doorbell ... I suppose that made my "ridiculous red earmuffs", as she referred to them during one painful conversation, pale in comparison.

We know that going it alone, being individual and standing out is a big no-no in Germany, so clubs also meet this need and enable you to blend into a crowd brought together by a common interest. This club mentality also reflects the deep German dislike of doing things by themselves. I'm astonished by the number of times someone posts on Facebook that they're looking to meet someone they can "get a beer with from a kiosk and just chill by the river". Or the number of times someone writes that they are currently drinking a beer in town and is anybody free to join them. Right this minute. Perhaps this is some kind of desperate attempt to come across as relaxed, casual and easy-going, but if that is really the case then it's seriously at odds with how Germans view friendships. Friendships are not to be entered into without consulting your diary and checking your availability for the year ahead. Should you wish to have a lasting friendship with a German you will need to be available to meet every Tuesday at 8 p.m. for deep and philosophical discussions where you are not afraid to "speak your mind" whether it's necessary or not, preferably with a cheap and warm take-out beer from a kiosk. A true German also considers activities such as ironing or watching TV to be concrete appointments with themselves, thus are inflexible. A friendship must under no circumstances be "superficial" and by superficial you should understand this means ad-hoc get-togethers at irregular intervals with someone with whom you do *not* share a common goal.

Even breaking the ice and getting to know a German is hard work. Not long ago I tried to strike up a conversation with a German friend of a friend in a café. I asked her what she did for a living. She replied, "I used to train university students to teach in primary schools."

That was it. End of conversation. She didn't return the question either. I struggled to bring the conversation round after that. Had she used a hole punch that was reserved for staff who sat in a different corner of the staffroom to her? Did she have an affair with a pupil's parent? Did she spit back on her colleague? I'll never know. I wondered if I was doing something wrong. Perhaps with this logic, if someone asks me my age (which they always do here), then I should reply, "I used to be forty-two."

Although making small talk about the weather is considered a British pastime, Germans love nothing better than a good moan about "*Biowetter*" or "bio-weather". Hypochondriacs abound in the so-called country of reason and order and all those years spent toughening yourself up at school are quickly forgotten once you're an adult and you think you'll get the bubonic plague if you run out in your dressing gown to your bin without dressing as if you're going on a polar expedition. If you come to Germany and feel out of sorts, be sure to check the daily "bio-weather" report to find out the mysterious answer to your ailment. Surely if you're feeling melancholic and down in the dumps it's due to the fact you are suffering from "*Frühjahrsmüdigkeit*" (spring tiredness) and not just because you've been verbally abused by a complete stranger yet again or ripped off by your internet company. Bio-weather affects people of all ages, and proves to be particularly prominent when you have a busy work schedule. A former teaching colleague, poor soul, was forced to take two weeks' sick leave after a holiday to Morocco due to the drastic temperature change back in Germany.

In Germany, going to the doctor's is also a national sport. Apparently, an average German goes to the doctor's a minimum of eleven times a year, the French six times and the Swedes three times.[59] According to statistics, 80 per cent of doctors' visits in Germany finish with a prescription, versus 42 per cent in the Netherlands[60], which is completely in keeping with the money mentality as doctors are paid to give out prescriptions. Although to be frank I wonder why they bother. I mean, the answer to most ailments tends to be along the lines of "do sport, drink lots of tea, wear a scarf 24/7 and don't open the windows". Germans also love a bit of melodrama and having something to obsess and be paranoid about; life is generally always in a state of "crisis" or "*Krise*" as it's known to Hermann. I bumped into an old colleague in town not long ago and I noticed he was looking quite pale and drawn. My first thought, obviously, was that he must be suffering from "spring tiredness" as it just happened to be 30 March. I asked him how he was and he said he was going through a "crisis". Even though I was rather taken aback by the strength of the word "crisis" I nonetheless probed for details. It transpired that he had recently had a few rows with his wife. How this constituted a crisis I'll never know as it was common knowledge that he had been living a separate life from his wife for years.

You see, for most Germans showing emotion is *verboten*, indeed, being labelled "emotional" puts a negative stamp on your character,

---

[59] *Leben in Deutschland*, Sommer, p. 188.

[60] *Leben in Deutschland*, Sommer, p. 188.

so that when a German *does* actually show emotion, it's completely over the top, and nine times out of ten over something trivial. German TV and film reflect this. I remember coming across a reader's letter in the magazine *Der Spiegel* about the legalisation of gay marriage in Germany and the fear that this would lead to all manner of degeneration within society, like, wait for it, *being allowed to marry your own dog*. Because if you can marry a member of the same sex, then surely the only logical conclusion to draw from this is that one day people will start marrying their pets. This extreme paranoia carries over to making or not making friends. The Germans call a stranger a *"Wildfremder"*, so there is an element of "wildness", hence danger, in befriending someone after the age of five. It is again *verboten* to start up a conversation with the woman you've been sharing your commute with for three years, it's simply not on to smile at a stranger and make a comment about the weather, terrible service, etc., but it is totally normal to ask a stranger online if they fancy grabbing a beer and going for a walk with you. I think I'll always feel lost in this country.

In a nutshell, it's really an uphill struggle making friends here and feeling part of a community. A couple of years ago we had the possibility of getting a kitchen at the vocational college with Herr Blockwart and co. Not only would that have been quite handy, there could have been a nice social aspect to it, too. It would have at least made a welcome change to seeing my colleagues sitting on their chairs, arms folded, heads down and eyes closed during lunchtime. But unfortunately, it was just not meant to be. About a week after we got the offer the first objection via email was sent round.

After a long and stressful day dealing with pupils, I don't want to be spending my only break washing up and cleaning.

More emails soon flooded in, along very similar lines, all objecting to having to tidy up, until one colleague chipped in and tried to save the day. She suggested a roster to save us from what otherwise could easily turn into complete and total anarchy. What we needed was a clear system where everyone knows when it's their day to clean up so they can plan their sick days accordingly. Without a clear set of rules to follow we would probably all have to resort to common sense, you see. "Well one day it might only be seven cups, but another day it could be several plates and bulky utensils too," said one colleague, totally enraged at the mere prospect of having more to clean than someone else. Whatever has happened to the much-lauded German sense of togetherness and solidarity, I asked myself. Nevertheless, the entertainment that I got from these email exchanges gave me a sense of courage I've never had since while working at the vocational college. I opened up my email account and typed a message of my own.

One day it might be twenty cups, several plates, bulky utensils and a spoon, and then where would we be?

Unsurprisingly the email exchange finished there and we never did see that kitchen.

CHAPTER 36

§161 Das Land der Dichter und Denker
The land of poets and thinkers

❧

B ut if you do somehow manage to make a friend as an adult there's a great chance it will be characterised by constant drama and clinginess, or, more commonly, theatrics. At the end of a long class one day, I was quite pleased with myself for having managed to get one of my more challenging students in touch with another student. I was hoping some kind of friendship could develop between them. My challenging student had a knack for linking the question to something totally unrelated, oftentimes forgetting there were other people in the class and thereby completely ignoring them while she drifted off into a monologue and completely detached herself from reality. She had made herself unpopular, in particular with the young Russian woman whose eyes would roll as soon as she had to listen to this student. The tension between these two students was vividly felt in the classroom and I often entered the lesson with a sense of trepidation and fear. This difficult student was also unemployed. Knowing the prejudice the unemployed are confronted with here and so wishing to help her, I suggested she go for coffee with another student, with whom I felt she might have things in common. When I asked her how her meeting went the following week, I was told that, though she enjoyed it she could never be friends with this woman. "But why not?" I asked. "You've just said that you had a nice time together."

"Well," the challenging student replied, "the thing is, she has a job and I don't." In other words, an unemployed person couldn't have a friendship with an employed person, presumably because they are not 100 per cent identical.

For some reason, perhaps because I had merely acknowledged her existence, this difficult student got a bit too clingy with me. It started off quite harmless, like having a five-to-ten-minute chat, or moan, after class. It then built up to long emails, where she told me about her ex-boyfriend with whom she still lived but who was trying to force her out, or about her job interview where she was told off for being too "direct". (She was told that she was "*forsch*" which Germans tend to use when one has been too direct, or "snappy". Being "*direct*" is largely viewed as a positive quality.) *Remember – Germans like to dish it out but they can't take it themselves.* It then went up a further notch following a message she sent me which implied she was suffering from domestic abuse. I couldn't just ignore this so I suggested we meet in town for a coffee so that she could tell me plainly and simply what was going on and we could look into alternative accommodation for her. We get to the café and she's looking happy and relaxed, so my first feeling is one of huge relief. We both order a hot drink and start talking. I keep waiting for her to mention the situation at home which she alluded to in her email, but she never does. I want to steer her towards this topic, but I can't get a word in edgeways. When I notice that I have finished my drink and she hasn't so much as taken a sip of hers, I realise that this woman is not in danger at all; she just desperately needs company and someone to talk to. When the subject of her boyfriend finally does come up, she makes no reference to feeling scared at home, rather she chooses to tell me that it's weird being taller than him. Two hours later when we leave the café, I make a sad but important discovery. The sheer strain of living in a country where everyone walks around with a face like a wet weekend and a personality to go with it makes it much more natural to cling to someone, even if it's only because they treat you with a modicum of respect or simply acknowledge your existence. It also goes some way towards explaining the German paradoxical personality; that you can be both so clingy yet so self-involved; so massively aggressive yet at the same time so cowardly. I simply must cite the wonderful George Mikes whose observations of the German character back in 1952 were just spot on:

They [Germans] have both learnt to be submissive and martial, sentimental and ferocious at varying times. They are both accustomed to swallow insults and then, when there is a chance, to erupt with the fierceness of a volcano. They both have reason for many justified complaints, and so they have become unable to forgo any opportunity of seizing on silly and unimportant wrongs.[61]

Just remember that dog poo.

Even my landlady Mrs Bouquet put on a convincing display of drama when she had a talk with me to give me my notice. While it's true that for five years or so we had got on well together without any hiccoughs, had enjoyed some highs – the occasional glass of wine and giggle, and the odd low – she picked me up from the hospital where I was stationed for five days – we were by no means ever bosom buddies. After she had spent some time criticising my lifestyle, in particular, my ghastly red earmuffs and my high heels which make a sound on the pavement, she suddenly and out of nowhere became nostalgic and tearful. She looked over at me, eyes red and filled with tears, and asked me who else in Germany had supported me like she had? Who else had been with me through thick and thin? Maybe this is what people mean when they refer to the Germans as a romantic nation – their sometimes absolute detachment from reality and the quickness with which they become upset, shouty, or rather completely inconsolable (watch any German film or programme to find out more). Germans are very quick to remind anyone who might be listening that in the nineteenth century they were famed as the land of "*Dichter und Denker*" (poets and thinkers). In the twentieth century they were famous for starting and losing wars, yet they don't bring that up in conversation. As far as I can see, however, this common type of behaviour is the sole relic of the period of "poets and thinkers".

Now I've never been on the market to date in Germany, can't for the life of me think why, but I have been set up, and boy was it memorable. The head of English at one of the universities I worked at, not the one whose breath could give a rotting corpse a run for its

---

[61] *Über Alles*, Mikes, Penguin Books, 1969.

money, said he had a spare ticket to the opera and would I like to join him, his wife and son. I'm not a massive fan of the opera but I'm not good at spontaneously declining offers when my only justification is I'd rather eat my own head than sit through the opera with people I don't know, so I smiled politely, thanked him, and said I'd be there. In the late afternoon, before the performance, we met up in town and had a coffee together. The wife greeted me by telling me I had put on weight since the last and only time she saw me, her husband, laughing awkwardly, said that he'd noticed I was a bit too fond of chocolate hence the weight gain (which I hadn't even realised), while the grown-up son moodily stared into space for the duration of the coffee. After the café we paid and went for a stroll. And then the dodgy thing happened. At the end of our little walk the husband stopped dead in his tracks, turned around to face me and his son, and casually said that he and his wife would now make their way to the opera; they'll see us after the performance. And just like that off they disappeared leaving me with several hours to kill with a man who had barely said five words to me all evening. He suggested we go for pizza so we found a nice-looking restaurant and did just that. Surprisingly, away from his parents he opened up and started making conversation. The evening is saved, I thought to myself. We had a little chat and then tucked into our pizzas. A few minutes into the meal the waitress came to our table and asked, as you do, if everything was OK with our meal. I said everything was lovely, but the son just pouted and said nothing. When she went away, he looked at me angrily and said, "Why should she care what my pizza tastes like? It's *my pizza." Remember – Germans have a particular understanding of and reaction to small talk and politeness.*

The Covid pandemic provided Germans with just the opportunity they've secretly been craving to boss people around big style and get just a little more hysterical than normal while doing so. It was great having clear rules thrust upon us, such as having to stand 2 metres apart. This means that your average German doesn't have to think for himself AND can waste no time yelling at you if you don't move out of their way when they want to push past you, or fight over the armrest with you between the seats on a train. Normally, in the pre-Covid days, hence when the concept of personal space was still non-existent, when out shopping in a German supermarket there were a few little games you could play with yourself to take your mind off either a) the view of the rotting vegetables that look like they should have been thrown out last week, or b) staff loading shelves very slowly in the middle of the afternoon, or c) the obnoxious person behind you ramming their shopping trolley up your backside. One game I call "Checkout Run". Here's how it goes: the first person to anticipate a new queue opening up makes a mad run to the front of the queue, pushing, elbowing and shoving past anyone who dares stand in their way. Bonus points may be awarded depending on how far back you were in the original queue. Use of elbows and other weapons, such as a handy cucumber or a fat wallet, is encouraged.

If you're particularly unlucky, you may find yourself dealing with a deadly combination of a robotic personality coupled with a dose of hysteria. Walking into my local supermarket one day, I was greeted by the sight of a middle-aged woman with her shopping trolley exiting the store at the entrance. Along I come, unarmed and content in my own little world, when a loud voice booms out at me:

"*Und WIE sollen wir das jetzt machen?*" "And *HOW* should we go about this?"

Clearly the sight of another human being, an obstacle on her path, was just too much to take. How dare I wish to shop at the supermarket at the same time as her! "Normally I let people exit before I enter," I answer, "but as you're standing in the wrong place and shouting at me like it's my fault, I'm going to walk in." I walk past her, maintaining enough distance so as not to make her have a heart attack, while also giving her the option to prepare herself and move. I never expected that to be the end of it, so it came as no surprise at all when I heard a screech of trolley wheels and footsteps behind me. The woman decided to follow me back into the supermarket.

"This lady is a danger!" shouts Ms Trolley-trash to the staff behind the meat counter. "You have to keep an eye on her!" she goes on.

The staff behind the counter didn't so much as flinch; they'd probably had similar scenes before. As she got no response, Ms Trolley-trash decided to leave. As luck would have it, no poor unsuspecting soul wished to enter this time.

CHAPTER 37

§371 *Gebildet oder eingebildet?*
Educated or conceited?

ᘏᗑᘏᗑᘏ

As everything in Germany is such a massive uphill struggle it's perhaps no wonder that Germans place so much emphasis on escaping in their precious free time. Carnival and its months-long planning is a case in point. This is the only time in the year you are allowed to have fun and throw caution to the wind. Hermann <u>will</u> have a jolly good time because he has noted this date in his diary six months ago. You can spot the German fondness for escapism in their love of dressing up and acting out fantasy role-plays. Germans think that the British love dressing up as we wear uniforms to school, but at least half the people I know here enjoying putting on their medieval gear once a fortnight and playing with their swords, or getting together to play a board game with a nice, clear set of rules and punishments. Though how the latter example constitutes escapism I'll never know. Yet when it comes to more intellectual and cultural pursuits, it's important that a) these are as realistic as possible, and b) they are dictated to you from a superior source. I once read an article with my students which provided an overview of the legal system in the UK. An Asian participant was surprised as they said that they hadn't seen court cases develop in this way in the British and American legal series they loved watching. Before I had time to think of something to say to this a German participant piped up and said that this is precisely the reason why German legal shows and court dramas are not popular with Germans; they are too far removed from reality. "Why would I want to watch something completely made up?" they went on to add. Another time I showed my students a clip of a recent Ken Loach film, *I, Daniel Blake*, about the benefits system in the UK. "I just don't understand why the director didn't use real people, people who are really living off benefits," was the response I got (for my sins I actually found out later that in most of his films Loach does actually use "real" people). The film had no impact, no power on my German audience, as it was made up.

The German love of being told what to think extends to what they read or watch. Especially if it makes them look intellectual. Whether or not the book or film is actually good seems to be irrelevant. Always on the lookout for a good read, I once asked a friend over a coffee if they were reading anything interesting at the moment. He told me he was about 100 pages into a book where so far, the main characters had gone for a walk. He admitted that it was painstakingly dull but he was determined to finish it regardless. I didn't get it, and he could see that from the expression on my face. He went on to explain in some detail that he watches the latest literary reviews either on a German talk show (don't even get me started on their endless talk shows) or consults the literature reviews in a newspaper to see what the bestsellers are, then chooses his books accordingly. "Ah!" I replied, as I couldn't think of anything nice to say to this. My friend was going to persevere with his dull as dishwater book as it would make him look well-read, and that's what matters after all.

If you don't own a television and don't read newspaper and magazine best-seller lists, how can you know what books to read? Well fortunately there is help at hand. Dotted around many towns and cities across Germany are open bookcases, the idea being that you can browse, take a book if you like the look of it, and ideally replace it with an unwanted book of your own. Germans see this as yet another shining example of their caring and sharing society, and the added bonus is they get hard-ons as it's all for free. I see it as a convenient way of getting rid of stuff you don't want that's cluttering up your flat. Oftentimes Germans portray themselves as a community-oriented and helpful society, always willing to help those less fortunate and act out of solidarity. Yet when horrific floods hit the beautiful Ahr Valley in July 2021, what did Hermann and many of his friends donate to help the victims? Carnival clothes. And while we're on the subject, if German society is so geared towards acting out of solidarity, why do civil servants not pay into one of the ninety-six health insurance providers and why are they exempt from paying pensions? Anyway, one afternoon I was browsing through one of these bookcases, quickly passing through all the 1970s travel guides and VHS cassettes when I came across a typically German-style aggressive note to all users of the bookcase. A certain user was very angry as one day they happened to deposit around twenty books only to find out that the very next day – shock horror – *all* the books had been taken! The note-writer could only deduce from this that one naughty individual had been very greedy indeed and had taken all the books for himself. I could only wonder why any of this mattered. Surely when you decide to get rid of items then they no longer belong to you, so it's no longer your business what happens to them, is it not? The mind boggles.

In Germany it is socially acceptable to read biographies, specialised books in you field of work known as "*Sachbücher*", non-fiction, detective stories and thrillers. *Remember – Quadratisch, praktisch, gut.* After all, in what other country would you expect to find on the best-seller list for years a book about your gut? Fiction is often considered as too frivolous, as is watching drama series on TV instead of documentaries (although since the arrival of Netflix even Germans have started to admit they enjoy something other than nature documentaries). Germans have coined a special word to lift fiction out of its frivolous category, "*Belletristik*". This translates as "high-brow" fiction, or literary works, and there is no social stigma involved in liking this. Once I remember my surprise when a group of students all aged sixty-plus revealed to me that they didn't know who David Bowie was. My lesson plan was centred around him, and they were sitting there asking themselves whether the song "Major Tom" rang any bells. Luckily after a few minutes of wondering two students said they vaguely knew it. It goes without saying that I then had to improvise for the remainder of the lesson.

CHAPTER 38

§925 *Weltführer Gesundheit!*
World leaders in health!

༄ஓஒ௸

Particularly during the extraordinary times of Covid-19, people, mostly Germans, were quick to remind me just how fortunate I was to be living in a country with fantastic health care and facilities. Indeed, the initial response to the crisis was clever. Early testing meant that there were far fewer fatalities here than elsewhere, and this also enabled us to get through the first lockdown relatively unscathed. The immediate response at least was spot on. Yet I haven't always felt so safe and in such competent hands (though I imagine I'm far more relieved than the patients of the more than thirty doctors and nurses who injected their patients with saline solution).[62] Moreover, we are still, three years on, struggling with a low vaccination rate compared to the rest of Europe and the UK. Germany has a strange system of health insurance, or more precisely, a nasty patchwork of ninety-six legal providers, with roughly 90 per cent of the population insured through public health insurance providers and the remaining 10 per cent on fully private coverage. This dual system of welfare exacerbates inequality and frequently undermines the quality of public services. The upshot of all of this is a fragmented, uncoordinated system with unrelated specialists all in their own little world (mind you, the same could be said for teachers, estate agents, tax advisors, the list goes on). Furthermore, Germany does not even have a cradle-to-grave patients' record system. What most

---

[62] https://www.theguardian.com/world/2021/aug/11/nurse-in-germany-suspected-of-replacing-covid-vaccines-with-saline-solution

expats don't seem to realise is that Germany does not have free health care as is the case with the NHS or the universal tax-funded health care of Scandinavian countries. When I took up my first position teaching at a university, I wasn't aware that my privileged employed status would grant me automatic access to a public health insurance provider with my employer sharing the costs with me 50/50. Getting into a health insurance scheme in the first place is, in fact, often a question of your employment status and I was luckily spared the confusing maze of rules, policies and options that so many other foreigners are confronted with.

Moving to a new country is stressful at the best of times, so it's little wonder that many of us don't realise that if you don't get public health insurance no later than three months after arriving in Germany, the health insurance providers have no obligation to take you. I find this somewhat at odds with the fact that having valid health insurance is a legal requirement here. This is where a former Business English student of mine from Mexico got caught out. Her health insurance ran out shortly before she suffered a quite severe sporting injury. When she tried to take out public health insurance she was rejected as she'd been living in Germany for a year but had all the while been insured back in her home country. Her only other option was to take out a so-called "basic tariff" (meaning that the provider has to accept everyone, no matter what) from a private insurer at the "bargain" price of 796 euros a month (maximum). Now if my student had been married, her partner could get a regular job with employee status automatically granting them membership with a public insurance provider, AND – now comes the really mind-boggling bit – get their spouse covered automatically for free.

In Germany it really pays to be married. You can get automatic and free health care for you *and* your child. Like in the US believe it or not, giving birth uninsured can cost you thousands even if there are only relatively minor complications. Being married also means you have far fewer taxes to pay as you can benefit from the wonderfully Stone-Age and rolls-off-the-tongue *"Ehegattensplitting"*, which roughly translates as "tax splitting for married couples". Unofficial partnerships do not count for tax purposes in Germany, perhaps because such modern thinking and open-mindedness might open the door to all sorts of chaos, such as marrying someone out of love rather than money, heaven forbid. That former colleague of mine, who I thought was suffering from "spring tiredness" but was just experiencing another "crisis", increases his salary by *a third* every year as his wife is the breadwinner and the discrepancy between their incomes is considerable. His tax bill becomes significantly smaller at the end of the tax year. The whole idea of this is that your total income is added, divided by two and both parties get taxed at the rate determined by the amount. In fact, the tax splitting for modern couples is really nothing other than a relic to former times when the woman stayed at home and perhaps did a couple of hours work a week just to get out of the house. In short, the married couple is never worse-off than two single tax payers. Indeed, an eye-watering 47.8 per cent of a single person's salary goes on taxes and duties. This sort of arrangement with a working husband and stay-at-home wife is still far too common in Germany nowadays and is even, dare I say, encouraged. Indeed, as one woman in an online forum so aptly put it, *"Why get married if it doesn't offer you a personal advantage?"* Whenever this topic comes up in newspapers many people are quick to point out that without this tax-splitting model there is no rational reason to get married. As if this kind of thinking isn't bad enough, the tax system only offers choice to married couples. Most couples here tend to opt for tax classes 3 and 5. They don't have to, but this combination affords them the greatest advantages just outlined. So married people are more equal than others in Germany it would appear. Below you can see how this tax was calculated in 2021 together with the rewards that will have been reaped.[63]

---

[63] Source: income tax calculator of the BMF, basic and splitting table for 2021.

Individual tax assessment (basic tax class)					Joint tax assessment (*Ehegattensplitting*)	Tax benefits
Partner A	Tax A	Partner B	Tax B	Total Taxes		
60,000 €	16,063 €	0 €	0 €	16,063 €	10,182 €	5,881 €
50,000 €	11,994 €	10,000 €	36 €	12,030 €	10,182 €	1,848 €
40,000 €	8,333 €	20,000 €	2,266 €	10,599 €	10,182 €	417 €
30,000 €	5,091 €	30,000 €	5,091 €	10,182 €	10,182 €	0 €

Let's now get back to that myth of affordable and effective health care for all. For those lucky enough to be a salaried employee, your boss pays half the insurance bill at roughly 8 per cent and the employee stumps up another 8 per cent. Students under thirty get a good deal, "only" having to spend round 70 euros a month, but freelancers and the self-employed are royally screwed. I remember once the battle that a self-employed wife of a friend had. A few years ago, she tried to open a no-frills bank account, but she was denied as her tax number revealed she was a freelancer. Apparently, this is *in Ordnung* in a social and modern democracy. In the end she was strongly advised to give up her freelancing activities and take up a position as a secretary so that her salaried status would make her eligible for public health insurance.

The reasons for which one can be denied something as crucial as health insurance you couldn't make up even with an imagination to rival Philip. K. Dick. But let's start off with the more "obvious" reasons for being denied this basic human right. Generally speaking, any psychological problem (especially something that sounds like depression or burnout) is a huge red warning for health insurance companies. Although transport cards and gym memberships are automatically renewed every year, health insurance companies don't always renew their contracts. At least not to a neighbour of mine (not the one without the bike helmet) after she was diagnosed with rheumatism. It's standard, therefore, to pay out loads in health insurance while at the same time half expecting that the insurers don't want to pay out for anything themselves.

When I had to get a dental implant following a nasty abscess and spent five days in hospital, I was delighted to find that my health insurance decided to cover 300 euros of the almost 3,000-euro treatment. Wonderful to see my health insurance has my back when I need it. Perhaps equally as galling as the huge sum I had to fork out for this abscess was the way in which it was dealt with. Back in August 2015 I started suffering almighty toothache. Not wanting it to get any worse I went straight to my dentist who recommend a cleaning (70 euros) and then an ibuprofen, extra strong, 600 milligrams, for the pain. I went for the cleaning and felt a short, sharp pang of pain around the sore tooth during the treatment, but didn't think too much of it. I then went to the chemist to get a "bargain" 4-euro pack of ibuprofen. Picking this up at the supermarket is not an option as supermarkets don't sell over-the-counter medicine as in the UK. And paracetamol and ibuprofen are fiercely expensive here, around 4 euros a packet. Shortly after this trip to the dentist the pain just got worse and my cheek started to swell. You'd think running around town looking like a sleep-deprived hamster would be enough for chemists and dentists to tell me I had an abscess and send me directly to hospital. But no; according to all the chemists I spoke to it would all be resolved with a cool pack and ibuprofen. When I couldn't take the pain any longer my mum persuaded me to make my way to the hospital. Once there a bright spark decked out in white from head to toe told me I had an abscess and would need to stay in hospital for up to ten days. Being in hospital wasn't so bad – if you discount being woken up at 8 a.m. every morning by the men in white coats doing their perfunctory rounds (it was at any rate the only time you got to see them). What really sucked was the time pre- and post-operation, which seemed to drag on interminably. After several weeks it was finally decided that the tooth needed to be extracted. My dentist couldn't do it himself, of course, so I had to be sent to a practice across town which specialises in pulling teeth. What my dentist could do, however, was draw up a list of medication to take before the extraction to ease the pain. When I added everything up it came to just shy of 100 euros. So, in the end I just stuck with the good old ibuprofen again. The tooth was then extracted and for a while everything was fine. Until that time when I went for another routine cleaning and left with a swollen lip and a tiny piece of cracked tooth. But apparently this is par for the course with dentists here, or so a student tells me who always comes out of the dentist's surgery with a lip to rival Leslie Ash.

I think the real double whammy in Germany is being female plus working freelance. The gender pay gap is already significant with women earning 18 per cent per hour less than men. Lawyers call this the "*Frauenveräppelungsgesetz*" which can be roughly translated as "law taking the mickey out of women". A recent documentary predicts that if things continue like this, one in three retired women will live in poverty from 2036. Even the middle class are affected, with women getting on average 46 per cent less pension than men.[64] The discrepancy here is considerable. German men get an average pension of 1,070 euros; German women a pathetic 809. People fare far better in the east, where women get 1,070 euros and men 1,141.[65] And it's not just women who have worked part-time who get peanuts as a pension; every third woman who has worked full-time for over forty years has too little pension. But as we know from this wonderful *Ehegattensplitting* law, women are not really encouraged to be active in the workplace, and the figures further confirm this, with 49 per cent of working women in Germany working part-time. One of the things that surprised me the most was the picture of Germany as a wealthy, successful nation, and the reality behind this image. This simply hides the fact that so many people are struggling. In many respects, walking around a city and watching the masses of middle-aged to elderly Germans rummaging in bins for plastic bottles they can get money for, reminded me of what the UK must have been like back in the early eighties. Those acting out that they are well-to-do but really don't have two cents to rub together and are desperate to hide it can be found all over the place. I often wonder how it's possible to pay so much for health care when

---

[64] *Rente. Grund für Altersarmut bei Frauen?* Released by NDR, 27.08.2021.

[65] To give you a point of comparison, here's how it works in Sweden. Employers pay more into the health insurance than employees (11.1 per cent versus 7.4 per cent), and there is a minimum pension of 820 euros which everyone is entitled to and which includes a rental allowance of up to 700 euros.

people are evidently struggling like this. According to a recent German documentary, it takes six-and-a-half generations to get out of poverty in Germany compared to two in Denmark and four in Spain.[66]

Only in Germany

A student of mine in a Business English course made an appointment with a chiropractor recently. She got there and ended up waiting for ages to see him as it turned out that he had double-booked himself. My student therefore only got to spend five minutes with him. In this time, he straightened her out (literally) but was unable to see to the second task as he said he was "too weak". The chiropractor then reassured my student and said that as he messed up the appointment schedule this "session" would be free of charge. Fast-forward a few days later and she receives a bill for 90 euros that she cannot contest.

If you join a private insurance scheme, let's assume because you're young and healthy, there is no voluntary way back into public insurance later on. German logic dictates that these rules are in place to prevent "free-rider" or "cherry-picker" problems where people use the private insurance with lower premiums as long as it's advantageous for them and when their situation changes and public is more attractive to them, they jump back. What's more, "old people" (people over the age of fifty-five in Germany who have been out of the state system for more than thirty months in the last five years), cannot re-enter the public system either. Even if unemployed. This would be seen as cherry picking and not at all acting out of "solidarity", i.e. only joining when you are more likely to need more care. This behaviour really riles Germans. Yet, paradoxically, they have no problems with "phantom" students signing up for university courses but not studying so they can get cheaper health insurance, child support allowance (*Kindergeld*), cheaper or free public transport and subsidised tickets to theatres, cinemas, etc. This is something that also only benefits the individual in question, and the tax/health insurance payer is left to make up for the low

---

[66] *Generation Hartz IV: Kinder kämpfen für ihre Zukunft.* Released by NDR, 31.05.2021.

contributions. Even universities know about this phenomenon but profess to have no problem with it.[67] What's more, the universities even argue that it's difficult to control this! So, what they really mean is that they can't be bothered to put in the work to investigate it.

Germany really does shoot itself in the foot with these complex and pricey health insurance options. A student of mine who works for an organisation dealing with researchers seeking to advance their careers and personal development by moving to Germany told us once that on too many occasions a promising post-doctoral student or junior lecturer has had to decline the invitation to come to Germany to work because they would not be able to bring their family along with them. This is down to expensive bordering on unaffordable German health insurance. Though it is just about possible to move to Germany as a single person and pay for health insurance, once these researchers factor in having to get health insurance for their entire family, they are priced out. As a result, Germany has failed and still fails to attract innovators in various fields of study.

For all the confusing insurance possibilities in Germany, a public policy expert at the Friedrich-Ebert Foundation believes that there is barely any difference in the level of care between private and public patients. Around 400,000 people in Germany can barely afford their private health care, most likely owing to the fact that they are paying up to 50 per cent of their income just for their health insurance. There are even thousands upon thousands of people in Germany not working at all, because their health insurance premiums would be too high for them to even take the first step into freelance employment. I for one see very little evidence of solidarity in such a system. Against this unjust background it's not surprising that there have been cases of doctors or retired doctors opening up surgeries to treat solely *uninsured patients*, despite my own GP telling me that no one is uninsured in Germany. In fact, an eye-watering 80,000 people are currently without health insurance. A recent report in *Stern* magazine interviewed an eighty-three-year-old retired doctor in

---

[67] https://www.faz.net/aktuell/karriere-hochschule/campus/scheinstudenten-warum-manche-sich-einschreiben-aber-nicht-studieren-13928373.html

Hamburg who receives around 6,000 uninsured patients a year, and contrary to what people may tell you here, these are not all the long-term unemployed. Many of these people are in fact German self-employed workers who had to cancel their private insurance when they went bankrupt.[68] It's little wonder that so many self-employed workers found themselves in this dire situation. Around 2010 all major German private health insurance companies introduced badly calculated "cheap" tariffs to draw the self-employed with low incomes out of the public health insurance. These cheap tariffs have since exploded in costs and thus brought thousands to the brink of bankruptcy. At the very root of this is a chaotic health insurance system and a serious lack of regulation of insurance advice (a bit like the problem with the German parasitic estate agents).

Because the Germans are so frustrated with their own way of life, they can be most nervous when foreigners also point towards traditions, habits and common practices which would be better forgotten. Like their practice of milking private health insurance patients for all it's worth. After all, private insurance pays higher fees to doctors, making their patients nice little cash cows for them. I've already put forward that Germans can be very creative when it suits them, and this can be seen once again in their dishonest billing, in particular for unnecessary treatments. By far the most common act of fraud committed by the medical profession here is to overcharge in foolish ways, such as itemising something on your bill which makes no sense whatsoever. What really took the biscuit here was when one of my private students told me that his private practice had snuck a fictitious treatment on his bill for 180 euros. It was fictitious because he wasn't even in Germany on the day when the supposed treatment took place. Guess what happened? My student took the doctor to court and won. Doctors have specialised software to optimise the invoicing and they have their staff trained for it. It's easy to see that doctors in Germany don't have to swear on the Hippocratic oath. They really can be greasier than a race track.

---

[68] https://www.stern.de/gesellschaft/ehrenamt/ehrenamt—internist-behandelt-menschen-ohne-krankenversicherung-30970396.html

In May 2023 after a break of several years, I got back in touch with my Polish sort-of-friend, Elmar. I had invited him out once just after the pandemic restrictions had been lifted, but being elderly and frail, he didn't want to risk going to a restaurant. So I waited a bit longer then decided to take him out to lunch in an old haunt of his, the cafeteria of the department store *Kaufhof* which boasts great views of the city centre. We met at the bus stop and as it was a weekend before May 2023, I could take him for free on my bus ticket. Straight away I noticed he was looking paler than usual, his eyebrow hairs seemed to have grown upwards, and he was angry to boot.

"I'm sure you've realised I'm not looking my best, even though I'm so happy to have some company for a change," said Elmar over the sound of the screeching brakes as we all jolt forward. "It's just that I'm so worried," he continued, "that I won't be able to fully enjoy it as there's so much on my mind."

"How have you been?" I ask, not wanting to confirm the fact just yet that he looks like death warmed up.

"I've been better. I haven't managed to see my GP in months, and not due to the pandemic." We jolt forward once again and I fear I'm going to slip off my seat. "My health insurance provider has blocked my card, although I am sticking to the monthly payment plan we agreed on together."

"*Das kann nicht wahr sein*," "That can't be true," mutters the man sitting behind us and not so discreetly eavesdropping.

"When I phoned them," Elmar went on, "they said they'd continue to block my card until I'm fully paid up."

"Are you sure you're not entitled to full coverage? I mean, you've been making repayments, just like you agreed." As he must be more than well aware of this himself, I go on, "When will you be all paid up?"

"That's the thing. In June, so only a few weeks away, but that's bad timing. Just my luck."

Before Elmar can elaborate, a sixty-something-year-old woman enters the half-empty bus, clocks us, and decides she'd rather cosy up to us than take one of the available twenty-odd seats. "*Rutschen Sie mal,*" she barks at me. "Move up."

Not wanting to make a scene in front of Elmar, I half-heartedly take my jacket off the empty seat and put it on my lap. Elmar gives me a raised eyebrow and awkward smile before continuing to pour out his woes, "We're coming up to the end of a quarter, and as I'm a state-insured patient, I don't have priority."

"You've lost me," I replied.

"Doctors pretty much shut their doors to state-insured patients at the end of each quarter, so in March, June, September and December, in order to make money with the privately insured. These are the times when doctors can increase their profit with those who have private insurance as they've pretty much used up all their budget and can't be bothered to treat patients who they can't make a profit out of."

I had to think about this for a few seconds. Most GPs shut up shop for the summer holidays, so this means that, broadly speaking, not only over July and August you're hard pushed to see a doctor, but also in June and September, so just before and after the long summer break. In my moment of stupefaction, I hadn't noticed that we'd just been sitting at a bus stop without moving for a few minutes while the middle set of doors opened and closed, opened and closed again, then opened and closed. It was like a noisy mirror of the doctor's surgery doors.

"Dear passengers, due to a technical fault you have to get off the bus here. A replacement is on its way." We finally get the news we're dreading from the bus driver so off we get and wait for the next one.

When we finally get to *Kaufhof,* Elmar is looking worse for wear. I get us some fish and vegetables and we sit looking out over the city while catching up on the last years of our lives. He starts to get some colour back in his cheeks and I feel that, despite the bumpy journey, he's glad he came out.

"Are you planning on staying in Germany for good?" he asks me.

"That's a good question," I say. "I love teaching, I love the content of my work, and, you know, being my own boss really isn't that bad."

Elmar chuckles to himself. "You want my advice?"

Remembering his wise words from one of the rare times we had a proper discussion, the warning not to take on everyone else's work, I nod my head eagerly.

"Consider life in Germany as a prison sentence. Keep to yourself, keep your head down, beat up people every once in a while to show them you're not to be messed with and they'll mostly leave you alone. And pay your reminders before you've been given the bills, even if you don't understand them."

Conclusions

༈

Living in Germany feels like someone has lifted up a giant rock to show me the unmentionables underneath; a health system which has slowly been falling apart for years, a pension system which is nothing more than a black hole, thousands of elderly people living hand to mouth and desperately trying to hide this fact, people looking for ways to cheat the system left, right and centre, because being entirely honest and transparent is too expensive, chaos and confusion everywhere because each and every *Bundesland* does things differently and there is no central organisation, and a transport system that has become a national joke. In short, living in Germany is a car accident in not-so-slow motion.

I have learnt that the Germany of 2005 in Lake Constance that I fell in love with wasn't the real Germany, or rather, the real German experience. As my stay had been completely organised by the British Council, my salary and insurances were automatically taken care of, I was, to a certain degree, leading a sheltered existence. It wasn't up to me to battle with various institutions to get what was rightfully mine, I never had to grapple alone with my tax declaration or move house, look for work, do everyone else's work, and hire an employment lawyer.

What has happened to Herr Blockwart and company?

Surely you must be asking yourselves what has happened to several of the people I've had dealings with here in Germany. Let's start with my personal spy. Herr Blockwart has been promoted and is now working as assistant headmaster. Ms Ticking-time-bomb, the only other English teacher at the vocational college, has been demoted, so to speak. Since the director of the school and her partner in crime "resigned", my former colleague has had her hours cut. It turned out that up until mid-2021 she was paid for seven hours of exam organisation every month, and this on top of her regular salary. As there's no way in the world she was spending that amount of time organising exams which took place every three months, Herr Blockwart axed her hours. I have no doubt whatsoever that her anger at this is being taken out on her colleagues as I write.

My replacement English teacher at the vocational college lasted a year. Prior to working there, she had eighteen years' teaching experience at a German *Gymnasium.* Yet one year only at the vocational college was more than she could take. I never met her, but I did send her a mock exam I once prepared as my former, charming colleague refused to share her materials. The director's position has yet to be filled.

Useless One at my first German university is still keeping busy by taking days off and ignoring her students and Mr Lowlife who bagged himself Useless Two's permanent position is taking even more time off sick than Useless One, or so former students tell me.

My empathetic students from the university of applied sciences are currently on their semester abroad. One young lady who supported my decision to quit my contract prematurely is now enjoying practising her French in the tropical island of La Réunion. I cannot help but feel immense pride for these former students of mine when I consider that they started their studies *online* during a worldwide pandemic, were robbed of many of the typical university experiences, lost their English teacher shortly before their exams, but are now spread out across the world immersing themselves in a new language, eager to make up for lost time while gaining vital skills for their degree and beyond. They really are a credit to us all.

Like my former students, I have also tried to move on. In October 2023 I started working at a new language school, which is targeted at learners 50 plus. I applied to the job advert in the paper and got an immediate phone call from the owner telling me that I'm basically too qualified to work there and I'd go crazy with boredom anyway, as most learners who sign up don't even have a rudimentary grasp of English. He ends up convincing me that I wouldn't want to work there so I think no more of the job, until a few weeks later when I get an email from the second owner of the company telling me how happy he would be if I could come and work for them. So, one Wednesday morning in October I go along to the school where I'm told that, because I'm so qualified, I can be given extra benefits!

These benefits boil down to being paid in vouchers and cash in hand. There's a wide range of vouchers I can choose from - supermarket vouchers, parking vouchers, cinema vouchers, restaurant vouchers; the list is endless. Being paid in vouchers can help me save on tax, you see, so this is all being done in my favour. I'm new to this kind of working arrangement as you can imagine so I ask for details, whereupon I get very long and complexly written emails along the lines of being paid up to 50 euros per month in vouchers and the rest in my account, and then whatever's left can be paid cash in hand. I have to read each and every email several times and very carefully as they're as clear as mud, but this seems to be the gist. As I'm trying to get to grips with this, owner number 1 comes back on the scene. At the end of October, he tells me that he's utterly flabbergasted as so many advanced learners of English have signed up for his courses. And here's the best bit – can I recommend any teachers who might be able to teach them?

The next thing for me to try and understand is how many hours I'll be teaching a week. There are 2 classes back-to-back I'm told. There is no paperwork, contract, list of participants and the like, but I start working anyway expecting these to be provided soon. After a few weeks of teaching, I notice that there's only one class, but when I try and press for details, I'm told that the owner himself doesn't know what's happening. That's why one Wednesday he proposes that we stay in the classroom at the end of the first lesson and listen to songs on his laptop while we wait for someone to turn up for the second class. Unsurprisingly, no one does. The following Wednesday I go to work to see a mug, apples and a bottle of wine on my desk with a Christmassy thank you message. Alarm bells start to ring as I fear that this is my salary for the month. I then check my bank balance for November - 60 euros worth of vouchers and 90 euros in my account. Not quite the 225 euros I was due for the 5 hours of teaching at 45 euros per unit. I write an email and attach an excel spreadsheet with all the calculations and data, but the owner doesn't respond. I just don't see how freelance teaching merits this amount of complication and stress. If I were haggling over the price of a carpet or trying to merge 2 businesses then fine, but for an hourly-paid job, this is beyond a joke. Alas, January 2024 will have to start with me leaving a job once more.

Regarding my personal life, my former landlady, Mrs Bouquet, the woman who called me out for wearing red earmuffs, has found herself a new tenant and has put the rent up by a whopping 150 euros a month for him. Meanwhile, in my current flat, I along with the other tenants are embroiled in battles with our landlady. We didn't have functioning heating or hot water for the best part of five months despite having had a hefty increase in ancillary costs.[69] For two weeks over Christmas 2022, it was so bad that the caretaker would come in every morning at 6 a.m. to manually fix the boiler. Replacing it would have been too expensive for the housing organisation, you see. And if that isn't worrying enough, I've recently discovered a crack appearing in the living-room ceiling. I know very well that if the roof falls in on me it would be my fault for mixing gravity and time. Is there really any end to the fun and games here?

Rules are still being creatively got around. Only the other day I was out walking in the forest when I saw a middle-aged woman jogging with her dog alongside her. The dog had a very long, bright orange lead on him, but this was unattached to his owner. The law stipulates that all dogs must be kept on leads. So, according to German logic, the woman was doing nothing wrong here, even if people ran the risk of accidentally stepping on the lead and choking her dog.

But it's the exceptions that have made it worthwhile here, and perhaps it's worth briefly mentioning these. First off, living close to the border and being able to travel around to different countries, each not much more than an hour away, offers a wonderful respite from the everyday stresses. Though at times I miss living in England, I never had so many travel options and such a variety of landscapes right on my doorstep. Second, I'm deeply grateful to have a wonderful and dedicated violin teacher with a myriad of tricks up her sleeve and bags of patience, and third, over the years I've built up

---

[69] Apparently one out of two utility bills in Germany contain errors, and one out of three people automatically expect to encounter difficulties with their landlords when receiving and paying them,
https://www.bz-berlin.de/berlin/jede-zweite-nebenkostenabrechnung-enthaelt-fehler

several rewarding and unexpected friendships. I also can't forget some of the main reasons I came to Germany in the first place – to experience the magic of the Christmas markets and to teach. And if it wasn't for my fabulous students, there's no way I'd still be here now.

How well do you know Germany? Answers

⌘

1. If Hermann invited you to a "public viewing", what might you expect?
   c) Watching live football in a bar or café.

2. How long does it typically take Hermann to complete a bachelor's degree in Germany?
   c) As long as he wants.

3. Until 2019, if Hermann was out of work, how would health insurance providers calculate how much he should be paying per month?
   b) They would make up a fictitious income of 2,232.25 euros for him. And Hermann would pay back around 16 per cent of that per month.

4. When is a *Deutsche Bahn* train considered as being late?
   b) If it arrives up to six minutes after the scheduled arrival time.

5. How much does Hermann earn per month if he has a so-called "mini-job"?
   a) 520 euros[70]

6. What does Hermann do to give himself a clear conscience?
   b) Separates his rubbish diligently when people are watching.

7. When does Hermann form an orderly queue?
   c) When purchasing an ice cream.

---

[70] At least you do not have to pay tax on this.

8. Why is Hermann afraid of turning fifty-five?
    a) Because it's the age at which it's nigh-on impossible to be accepted by a health insurance provider.

9. On average, how many times does Hermann go to the doctor's per year?
    c) Eleven times.

10. Hermann is considered to be pretentious if he does which of the following?
    b) Wears elegant clothes.

11. Which services does Hermann get for free in German banks?
    c) None of the above.

12. When Hermann meets a graduate in the field of engineering who works as a graphic designer, what thoughts might go through his mind?
    c) Why did this person fail as an engineer?

13. What does having "self-reliance" and "confidence" mean to Hermann?
    a) Telling people explicitly what you need and want.

14. What is the approximate average monthly pension for a single woman in West Germany?
    c) 800 euros

15. Hermann likes to make sure he fits in with his fashion. What is he most partial to wearing?
    b) Trousers ending roughly around his ankles with several centimetres of sock visible.

16. How can you tell whether Hermann is "acting out of solidarity"?
    a) He doesn't take up freelance work.

17. How many state health insurance providers are there?
    c) More than ninety.

18. What is Hermann's understanding of "community"?
    b) Being a member of one or more of the 87,000 organised clubs.

19. How long can Hermann teach at universities on temporary contracts before he must stop or face breaking the law?
    b) Six years.

20. How much interest can Hermann typically hope to earn on his savings?
    c) A maximum of 0.20 per cent.